INHERIT THE KINGDOM

Meditations on
The Sermon on the Mount
(originally *The Directory of the Devout Life*)

F.B. MEYER

Though this book is designed for
the reader's personal enjoyment and
profit, it is also intended for group
study. A Leader's Guide with Victor
Multiuse Transparency Masters is
available from your local bookstore
or from the publisher.

VICTOR
BOOKS a division of SP Publications, Inc.
WHEATON. ILLINOIS 60187

Offices also in
Whitby. Ontario. Canada
Amersham-on-the-Hill. Bucks. England

Unless otherwise noted, Scripture is quoted from the *King James Version* (KJV).
All other Bible quotations are from the *American Standard Version* of 1901 (ASV).

This book was originally published by Fleming H. Revell Company in 1904.

Recommended Dewey Decimal Classification: 226:21
Suggested Subject Heading: BIBLE N.T.—SERMON ON THE MOUNT

Library of Congress Catalog Card Number: 84-52038
ISBN: 0-89693-396-2

VICTOR BOOKS
A division of SP Publications, Inc.
Wheaton, Illinois 60187

CONTENTS

PREFACE

There is too much of mere sentiment and emotion in what goes by the name of Christianity, and too little practical Christian living. The tree is not good, the inward parts are not thoroughly cleansed, the rule of Christ is not absolutely dominant in speech and life. People are willing enough to accept freely a forgiveness which He purchased by His blood, but are slow to believe that He is a King whose Law must be obeyed in its jots and tittles.

We can never allow the great objective facts of Christianity and their attendant doctrines to sink low on our horizon, but we must give equal prominence to the demands of Christ for a righteousness which shall exceed that of the Scribes and Pharisees, and a perfection which shall resemble that of God. We have no right to be content with saying "Lord, Lord." We must also do the things which He says.

In my earliest days I was reared in a school that loved the "juicy" doctrines of Grace, and if a sermon were preached from our pulpit which laid special stress on Christian ethics, during our walk home it would be dismissed as Luther dismissed the Epistle of James, as "right strawy," and as savoring too much of the moral essay and too little of the Gospel. It seemed as though some in the audience were a little afraid of Christ as a teacher of morals, while willing enough to recognize Him as Saviour.

We understand the matter better now, and have learned that those who would ascend the hill of the Lord, and stand in His holy place, must have clean hands and pure hearts, must not lift up their souls to vanity, nor swear deceitfully (Ps. 24:4).

Of course, the right kind of obedience is impossible apart from the Cross and the Spirit. We must be reconciled before we can become obedient children; we must be filled with the Spirit before "the fragrance of Christ" can be manifested through us in every place. The Sermon on the Mount must be read in the transfiguring light which shines backward from the later events in our Lord's life.

When, however, this is borne in mind, each sentence of that marvelous discourse glistens with celestial radiance and rings with the music of the Gospel. In such a spirit let us address ourselves to the study of the Sermon on the Mount, as it is contained in Matthew 5, 6, and 7.

F.B. Meyer 1904

INTRODUCTION

(Matt. 5:1-2)

Accompanied by His newly acquired disciples, our Lord traveled throughout Galilee, hastening from place to place, from one synagogue to another. Everywhere He proclaimed the Glad Tidings of the Kingdom, and accompanied the preaching by mighty deeds. He healed the sick and cast out demons, dispelling every form of infirmity and disease which He encountered in His triumphal progress. On the sunlit path of the Prince of Life all the sad results of human sin fled as the wreathed mists of morning before sunrise.

It was a morning without clouds. His fame spread far and near throughout all Syria. The people, who, between the exactions of the Pharisees and the hairsplitting of the Scribes, were like harried sheep, welcomed His advent with a great outburst of joy. On the one hand He was so accessible in His sympathy; on the other so transcendent in His purity and grace.

A general impulse of hope and expectation was diffused abroad, and they sought out all who were sick and diseased in mind and body, to bring them into His gracious and health-giving presence. In addition to these crowds of sympathizers and friends were groups of curiosity-mongers and sightseers, of inquirers and devout souls, who followed Him, with a great expectancy in their hearts, from Decapolis, Jerusalem, Judea, and beyond Jordan.

When He saw the crowds increasing thus, He felt that He must withdraw temporarily from their presence. He could not permit the seasons of holy fellowship with His Father to be broken in upon even by eager appeals for sympathy and healing. Besides, He had reached a decisive moment in His career, when, as His answer to the increasing malice of the leaders of Judaism, it became necessary to organize His followers, and secure the consolidation and perpetuation of His work. A forward step was to be taken, which demanded that He should give Himself to prolonged intercessory prayer, so that He might do nothing of Himself, but only what He saw His Father doing. He was to choose the men whose names, long afterward, were to be engraven on the foundation stones of the New Jerusalem. He must, therefore, give Himself to prayer.

The scene of this midnight vigil, and afterward of the Sermon on the Mount, is an upland rather than a mountain, which rises to about a thousand feet above the level of the sea, and is distinctly marked out from neighboring eminences by the two horns which crown its summit.

Let us follow the Master's steps as He ascended by a long and easy slope of unfenced common land, the grass of which was embroidered with daisies, white and red anemones, blue hyacinths, and the yellow-flowered clover, on which the brown cattle browsed. After a gradual ascent of three or four miles He reached at length a great crater-like space, with a slightly hollow floor, set in a frame of rough crags, and strewn with boulders and fragments of black basalt—as if they had been rained on the earth in a terrific shower (Dr. C. Geikie). Above, the hill rose up into two high, grassy knolls, some sixty feet in height, known as the Horns of Hattin. This is the spot, so tradition says, where the Master continued all night in prayer to God. He may have selected for His oratory the summit of one of those grassy knolls, while the disciples occupied some lower ridge; and at dawn the people began to gather from the neighboring villages, where they had spent the night, to crowd the vast audience chamber, hollowed out as an amphitheater below. On the southwest the huge cone of Tabor; to the north the majestic snow-crowned summit of Hermon; below to the east the glittering waters of the lake; far away on its other side the precipitous cliffs of Gadara, rising sheer from its shores; no signs of human habitation;

no sound of earthly toil; no fear of intrusion save from the feathered and furred denizens of air and earth, the free pensioners with the lilies on His Father's care—such was the oratory, whose soft grass was trodden by those blessed feet or indented by that kneeling form.

It was on the mountain, as Luke tells us, that He prayed (Luke 6:12-13). As the dawn broke over the hills He *called* His disciples from their slumbers, and chose from them twelve, that they might be with Him, and that He might send them forth to preach, and to have authority to cast out demons (Mark 3:13-15). He then appears to have sat down, after the recognized Eastern fashion, opened His mouth, and taught (Matt. 5:1-2). Through paragraph after paragraph, which were to mold the minds of people after a new fashion, and influence the course of coming centuries more powerfully than those of Plato and Aristotle, His speech moved with the transparency and brightness of the River of Life which proceedeth from the throne of God and of the Lamb. Then, descending with His chosen band of Apostles, and accompanied by the rest of His disciples, He descended to the level place where the vast congregation was awaiting Him, and lifting up His eyes with special tenderness on the inner circle, but in tones audible to the farthest extremities of the crowd, He repeated in a shorter form the marvelous discourse which He had already delivered (Luke 6:17-38).

This discourse, laying the foundation of the Kingdom of Heaven, may also be called the Directory of the Devout Life, and we can wish for nothing better than to drink into its spirit, and realize its exquisite ideals. While it is, in a literal sense, "the Sermon on the Mount," because it was uttered on one of the great natural altars of the world, may it not also be called so in the symbolical and metaphorical case? Our Lord was standing on the very summit of spiritual experience. His own soul was fragrant with the Beatitudes which He uttered for His disciples. He possessed in living human experience all that He inculcated. With exquisite naturalness and simplicity He was describing His own experiences, was revealing the secrets of His deepest nature, and was delineating in colors that can never fade the features of His own face. From the heights He was calling to people in the lowlands of error and sin, to summon them to His own standpoint. This is emphatically the sermon of the mountain heights.

The Old and New Covenants

The close similarity and contrast between this sermon and the giving of the Law from Sinai has often been discussed, and we need do no more than note the points that have been made. *There* the great prophet of the Old Covenant received God's Law by the mediation of angels, and his feelings must have been elevated far above their ordinary level; *here* the Prophet of the New Covenant utters the revelation of God from the depths of His own heart, from the matured experiences of His own habitual condition. *There* the Law was accompanied by the roll of thunder and the blinding lightning flash; *here* the accompaniments were soft breezes, the blue canopy of heaven, the lilies, and the birds of the air. *There* the Law was written on tablets of stone; *here* on the fleshly tablets of the heart. *There* the Laws were Prohibitions; *here* Beatitudes. *There* the first tables of the Law were shattered because of the disobedience of the people, and the second form was equally stern and exacting; *here*, out of tender compassion for the weakness of the people, our Lord repeats the sermon with a somewhat slighter texture. Moses constrained to obedience by pronouncing the disobedient accursed, while Christ attracts to loving loyalty by pronouncing the blessedness of the citizens of His Kingdom. People were not to be driven by terror, but attracted by winsomeness and sweet reasonableness.

This was the third discourse. The first had been to Nicodemus, the master in Israel, on the necessity of a spiritual union with God—this is the beginning of the devout life. The second had been to the unnamed woman at Sychar's well on the nature of spiritual worship—this is the nurture of the devout life. The third is on the rule and direction of the healthy and holy soul—this may therefore be called the Directory of the Devout Life. It has been said that there is nothing of the Cross or of Pentecost in this discourse; but each of these is required to transform these

10

precepts into living and gracious experience. There must be for each sinful soul that forgiveness and cleansing which are possible only through the blood of the cross, or it can never enter through the white gates of pearl into this city of God. For each, too, there must be the inbreathing of the new life—the being born again, not of corruptible seed, but of incorruptible—before that life can be cultured and molded into the developments of which this Sermon gives outline and model.

"How," asks the disciple in one of old Jacob Behmen's treatises, "shall I be able so to live as not to lose the eternal peace amid anxiety and tribulation?" To which the Master answers: "If you do once every hour throw yourself by faith beyond all creatures into the abysmal mercy of God, into the sufferings of our Lord, and into the fellowship of His intercession, and yield yourself fully and absolutely thereto, you shall receive power from above to rule over death and the devil, and to subdue hell and the world under you." Yes; and we may add, then you shall be able to realize the noble ideal which is presented in our Lord's incomparable Sermon on the Mount, as presented in these chapters.

OH, THE BLESSEDNESS!

(Ps. 32:1; Matt. 5:1-2)

There is a condition of soul which may be experienced and enjoyed by every child of our race, which the Master calls Blessedness. He uses the same words to describe it as is employed to set forth the Being of God and the Life of the Saints who have passed beyond the veil.

Blessed are ye (Matt. 5:11).

The glorious Gospel of the Blessed God (1 Tim. 1:11).

Blessed are the dead which die in the Lord (Rev. 14:13).

This condition of soul, however, need not be postponed until we too, in our turn, pass the Gate of the City, and find ourselves amid the solemn troops and sweet societies of eternity. It may be entered here and now. The fragrance of this garden steals through the crowded and noisy cities of our modern civilization like the morning air laden with the scent of new-mown grass. The gates of this City stand open, night and day, for lonely souls, in country and sequestered places, where the noise of our city life cannot reach, and at any moment they may tread its thronged streets, listen to its murmured speech, and join in its vast convocations, of which it is written: "Ye are come unto

13

Mount Zion . . . the City of the Living God . . . to an innumerable company of angels, to the general assembly and church of the firstborn" (Heb. 12:22-23).

How to Be Blessed

Blessedness does not depend on outward possessions, such as worldly goods, or lands, or high birth, or erudite culture. Indeed, there are words of Christ which suggest that they who stand possessed of these things will find it harder to enter that Paradise which has not yet faded from our world, and to pass through the gates of that City which are before our eyes, if only they were opened to discern them. When He repeated this Sermon of the Mountain Heights and of the Dawn, to the multitudes that stood breathless beneath its spell, He said, "Woe unto you that are rich . . . Woe unto you that are full . . . Woe unto you that laugh" (Luke 6:24-25). He did not mean that such would be necessarily excluded, but that entrance into blessedness would be harder for them; as when, after dusk, a camel strives to get through the needle-eye gate, placed in the city wall for belated pedestrians.

There is no human soul so illiterate, so lonely, so poor in this world's goods, so beset with hereditary sins and demonic temptations, that may not at this moment step suddenly into this life of blessedness, begin to drink of the river which makes glad the City of God, the holy place of the tabernacles of the Most High. It is not necessary to ascend into Heaven to bring it down, or to descend into the Depth of the Abyss to bring it up; it has not to be wrestled with or wept for; it is not to be obtained by the merit of holy deeds or as the reward for devoted service; it is not a garland which comes after long years in the council chamber or on the tented field. We have not to do, or feel, or suffer, but only to be; to cultivate certain dispositions; to possess a nature, here carefully defined—and instantly blessedness begins, an earthly light breaks on the soul, which is destined to increase into the full radiance of Heaven's high noon. "Come in, thou blessed of the Lord [can you not hear the angel voices?]; wherefore standest thou without?" (Gen. 24:31)

Jesus' Peace, Joy, and Love

Our Master did not speak of this condition of soul by hearsay; for thirty years it had been His sweet and deep experience. During His life in Nazareth had not the Lamb of God lain in His Father's bosom? Had He not realized that He was wrapped around with the love which had been His before the worlds were made? Had He not been content to let the great ones of the world go on their way of pomp and pride, because He was assured of a deeper joy, a more perfect peace, a more satisfying happiness than Caesar's smile or the Imperial purple could afford? The well of water was springing up in His own pure heart before He spoke of it to the woman at Sychar's well. He knew the Father, loved the Father, fulfilled His Father's behests, rested in the Father's will, was encompassed with the perpetual sense of the Father's presence, breathed the sunny air of the Father's love. During His earthly life, as He confessed Himself, the Son of Man was, therefore, already "in heaven" (John 3:13). He offers us what He was experiencing for Himself. "*My* peace I leave with you; My peace I give unto you" (John 14:27). "These things have I spoken unto you, that *My* joy might remain in you" (John 15:11), "that the love wherewith Thou hast loved *Me* may be in them" (John 17:26).

Not to the same degree, but after the same quality and kind, we may know in this life, amid difficult, tempestuous, and sorrowful experiences, what the Lord felt when He said: "He that sent Me is with Me; the Father hath not left Me alone, for I do always those things which please Him" (8:29).

Eight Ingredients of Blessing

The ingredients of this experience are enumerated thus:

(1) *It is blessed to belong to that invisible kingdom* which is already in our world, including within its ever-expanding circle all gracious souls of every race and age, breathing the ozone of Heaven into the stale and exhausted atmosphere of the world; its King the Enthroned Lamb; its subjects, the childlike, the forgiving, the gentle, and the pure; its laws, love; its advances, soft, sweet, irresistible as the dawn; its

duration, eternal. It is a blessed thing to know that one has the franchise and freedom of that kingdom, that one need never go out from its holy and strong embrace, and that men like John the Divine may greet us thus: "Your brother and partaker with you . . . in the . . . Kingdom . . . which [is] in Jesus" (Rev. 1:9, ASV).

(2) *It is blessed to be comforted with the comfort which only God can give.* When the eyes are wet with tears that refuse to be staunched, to feel a hand soft and strong wiping them away, and to discover that it is the Hand

> That can ruffle an evening calm,
> And bears Calvary's mark on its pierced palm.

When the face is buried deep amid the dried flowers and leaves of departed joys, to hear a whisper which thrills the sense, growing fuller and clearer like a flute, and to detect in its syllables the assurances of the Comforter Himself; when the sepulcher seems to hold all that made life worth living, to become suddenly aware that there is a Presence near at hand, and to find that the Gardener Himself is at hand to lift the drooping plant of life unfurling its petals again to the light; to be strong in God's strength, comforted with the paracletism of the Paraclete, to drink of the brook by the way—here is blessedness which eye hath not seen, neither the ear of ordinary people heard, nor the unregenerate heart perceived (1 Cor. 2:9-10). Even the bereaved and lonely heart, sitting amid the wreckage of all its joys and hopes, may be aware of this.

(3) *It is blessed to inherit the earth.* When that condition of soul is reached of which the Master is speaking,

> Heaven above is softer blue,
>   Earth around is sweeter green;
> Something shines in every hue
>   Christless eyes have never seen.

There is a new rapture in common sights, a new meaning in common sounds; lilies are robed more sumptuously than Solomon; the winged and furred denizens of the woodlands become, as St. Francis found them, "little brothers and sisters." As Cowper said, such a person may be poor compared with those whose mansions glitter in his sight, but he calls the luxuriant prospect all his own. Every wind wafts him blessing; all things work together for his good. Whether Paul, or Apollos, or Cephas, or the world, or life, or death, or things present, or things to come—all things bring their tribute to the one who has learned Christ's secret, which, like the fabled philosopher's stone, turns everything into gold. What inheriting the earth means is shown in the words of one of Christ's most proficient pupils, when he said: "I have learned in whatsoever state I am, therewith to be content" (Phil. 4:11). You may own vast estates, and get nothing from them. You may have no rod or perch of land, and yet you may derive joy and delight from every scene, and extract nutriment from every incident. Newspapers, public events, journals, travels, pictures, architecture, literature, human life—all shall minister to your joy and perfecting.

(4) *It is blessed to be filled.* In this life, as well as in the next, it is possible to hunger no more, neither thirst any more. Not to hunger for the husks that the swine eat, because filled with the provisions of the Father's table! Not to thirst for the fountains at which the children of the world seek to quench their thirst, because the well of water, that springs up to eternal life, is within! Not to clamor for the fleshpots of Egypt, because there is so plentiful a provision of manna. Oh, it is a blessed thing to be filled with the Spirit, to be full of joy and peace, to be fulfilled with God's grace and heavenly benediction, to be filled with the fruits of righteousness, to be filled with the knowledge of His will, to be filled unto the fullness of God. Tennyson says that the babble of the Wye among the hills lasts until the tidal wave fills up its channels to the brim; and the heart is restless till it is full—but when it has realized this blessed fullness, dipped deep into the fullness of God, and lifted out dripping with flashing drops, ah, then, evil has no lure to charm, the fear of man cannot intrude, the charms and blandishments of sense are neutralized. What more can the soul want than to be filled with Thee, O God, who did

make us for Thyself? Cannot a flower be satisfied which has a sun to shine on it, and a glacier-fed river to water its roots?

(5) *It is blessed to be the recipient of mercy.* There is never a moment of our lives in which we do not stand in need of mercy, both at the hands of our fellows, and, above all, from the hand of God. There is no saint in the heavenly Kingdom who does not, at some time or other, need to appropriate the petitions of the man after God's own heart, and say, "Have mercy on me, O God, according to Thy loving-kindness, according unto the multitude of Thy tender mercies" (Ps. 51:1).

We need mercy from little children, startled by our harsh tones; mercy from our employees, hindered by our inconsistencies, our quick temper, and imperious tones; mercy from husband or wife, brother or sister, neighbor or friend—above all, mercy from the Most Merciful; and it is blessed to know that we have it in Heaven's own measure, full, pressed down, and running over. So far from it making us lax in permitting sin, it predisposes us to more mercy toward the failings of others, more mercilessness to ourselves.

(6) *It is blessed to have the vision of God.* Not to terrify, as when Moses hid his face, and Elijah went into the covert of the cave, and John fell at His feet as dead; but more after the fashion of Mr. Hewitson's experience, when he says: "Our Redeemer is no mere abstraction, no ideality that has its being only in our shifting thoughts—He is the most personal of all persons, the most living of all who live. He is 'the First and the Last, and the Living One.' He is so near us, as the Son of God, that we can feel His warm breath on our souls; and as the Son of Man He has a heart like these hearts of ours—a human heart, meek and lowly, tender, kind, and sympathizing. In the Word—the almost *viva voce* [live voice] utterance of Himself—His arm of power is stretched forth beside you, that you may lean on it with all your weight; and in the Word, also, His love is revealed, that on the bosom of it you may lay your aching head, and forget your sorrow in the abundance of His consolation. To the Living One who died we must look that we may be

weaned and won over to God, that we may be strength-
ened, spiritualized, and sanctified." Who would not desire
a life like this, in which God should be the one dear
Presence, the one familiar and ever-present Object of
thought, the Friend with whom an increasing dialogue is
maintained. A young girl employed in a shop told me the
other day that her consciousness of God and her conversation with Him had now lasted for three years, and that
difficult things had become easy, as though He arranged all
and smoothed out the creases.

(7) *It is blessed to be recognized as a child of God.* Some are
undoubtedly children of God, who are not like God. It
would require a good deal of scrutiny to detect His image
and superscription on their face, or the tones of His voice in
their speech. The manners of the Heavenly Court are not
evident in their demeanor; the courtesy and thoughtfulness
that characterized the Son are not characteristic of their behavior to the poor and timid, to little children and women.
They too often break the bruised reed and quench the
smoking flax; they strive and cry and cause their voices to
be heard in the street; they do not bear, believe, hope, and
endure all things, and elicit the love of people to Him
whose name and nature they bear in every lineament. Be it
ours to be imitators of God as dear children, to be harmless
and blameless, the sons of God, without rebuke—to be thus
is to be blessed.

(8) *We come back to the Kingdom of Heaven.* Because blessedness is like a spiral staircase, we are always coming back
to the same standpoint from a higher position on the cir-
cling round. When we begin to live for God we find ourselves in the Kingdom, and are ravished with the beauty of
the dawn; but after years have been spent in doing His will
and walking in His fellowship there is a new depth of loveliness and significance in its infinite and Divine contents.

O Christ, Thou King of Glory, uplift us above the common dusty road of mortal life—lift us into Thy life, above
the heads of our enemies, above the weight of our flesh,
above the glamour of the world, and make us most blessed
forever, and glad with joy in Thy presence!

CHAPTER TWO

THE PASSIVE SIDE
OF THE BLESSED LIFE

(Matt. 5:3-6)

Let us study our Lord's ideal of character with the prayer that He would graciously repeat it in us, and that He would be in us that which He commends; for it is only as He gives us Himself in all the fullness of His perfected manhood that we can *apprehend* that for which we were *apprehended* (Phil. 3:12), and be that which He desires. Do you realize this, my reader? Have you made room for Him, and are you allowing Him to possess you wholly, till He becomes in very deed *your life*? A vine must abide in its branch, or fruit-bearing will be impossible. Apart from Him we can do "nothing" (John 15:5).

Blessed Are the Poor in Spirit

To be *poor in spirit* (Matt. 5:3) is to be vacant of self and waiting for God. To have no confidence in the flesh; to be emptied of self-reliance; to be conscious of absolute insufficiency; to be thankfully dependent on the life energy of the living God—that is poverty of spirit; and it has been characteristic of some of the noblest, richest, most glorious natures that have ever trodden the shores of Time. Happy are they who are conscious of a poverty which only the Divine indwelling can change into wealth, and who are willing, like the wondrous beggar of Meister Eckhart, to confess that they would rather be in hell and have God, than in heaven and not have Him.

It is, indeed, remarkable that some of the most richly dowered in mental and moral wealth have been most eager to confess that they were nothing—babes in the world of being, children picking up stones on the shores of boundless oceans, scholars on the lowest form of the school, to whom mature growth and knowledge seemed as yet indefinitely distant.

The way to become poor in spirit is to realize that you have no power of your own by which to bless and help others, and to open your whole being to the incoming and through-flowing of the wealth of the ever-blessed God. It was thus that the Master Himself lived and wrought. Though He was rich in all the Divine plenitude of His Divine nature, "He became poor" (2 Cor. 8:9) "and emptied Himself" (Phil. 2:7, ASV). In other words, He determined not to speak His own words, follow His own scheme and plan, or work His mighty works in His own might, but became the channel and instrument through which His Father spoke, wrought, and reconciled the world unto Himself. O soul of man, there is no other course for you and me! Not to draw up the water with which to quench people's thirst from the depths of our own souls, but to be channels through which the river of God may flow, as the water of faraway lakes is brought to the myriads of our great cities. To confess that you are nothing, but that Christ is all; to know that you can do nothing effective to bless people, but that Christ can, and will, do it by you—that is the secret of this poverty of spirit which unlocks the treasures of the Kingdom of Heaven.

Blessed Are the Meek

Many ancient authorities place *meekness* (Matt. 5:5) next, and it seems the natural order, for a soul that realizes its own nothingness and helplessness is likely to be meek. The meek are so occupied with their desire that God's grace should pass through them to their fellows that they are prepared to sink all considerations of their own standing and position so long as nothing may interfere with the effect for which they long. Their only thought is to carry their point, to bless people who do not want to be blessed, to vanquish hate by love, and rebellion by loving-kindness and tender mercy. They cannot afford, therefore, to be always standing on their own dignity and defending their own rights. These are willingly cast into the furnace to augment the flame, that the obdurate metal may be fused. "Being reviled, we bless; being persecuted, we endure; being defamed, we entreat. We are made as the filth of the world, the offscouring of all things" but "all things are for your sakes, that the abundant grace might through the thanksgiving of many may redound to the glory of God" (1 Cor. 4:12-13; 2 Cor. 4:15).

The way to become meek is to be absorbingly taken up with the love of Christ for you. Be lowly before God, allowing His love to enter and fill your heart, and you will find it easy to be meek toward people. Your pride will be driven out by the expulsive power of the new affection. You will be prepared to accept flouts and sneers, if only you can bless and help others; even as God who answers not the blasphemous and hard things that are said against Him, but continues to send His rain and cause His sun to shine to bring people back in penitence to His heart.

It would be a great mistake, however, to suppose that the meek are cowardly, deficient in strength of purpose or force of will: they are among the strongest and most strenuous of people. But they are strong in patience and strenuous in seeking the salvation of others. Let the cause of righteousness, justice, or truth be in question, none are so unbending or stalwart as they. Of the wrongs done to themselves they are disposed to take no count, but they dare not refrain from bearing witness, both by speech and act, whenever the sacred majesty of truth is assailed and in danger of being trampled underfoot.

Blessed Are They that Mourn

It is natural that the meek should become those that *mourn* (Matt. 5:4). They feel keenly the evil of sin and the sanctity of sorrow; like Him who sighed as He touched the

22

tongue of the dumb, groaned as He came to the grave of His friend, and wept as He beheld the city.

Of all mourners, Jeremiah is one of the most plaintive. There is no lyric on the page of history to be compared with the Book of Lamentations:

"Mine eye runneth down with rivers of water" (Matt. 3:48).
"Mine eye poureth down and ceaseth not" (Matt. 3:49, ASV).
"Mine eye affecteth my soul" (Matt. 3:51, ASV).

When we turn from the sin of the world, the woes of men, the high-handed wrong of the great, and the abject poverty, sorrow, and anguish of heart of the oppressed—to the sin of our own hearts, the broken ideals, the frustrated purposes, the perpetual contrast between what we would be and what we are, surely our tears must have more salt in them, and cut deeper courses in their flow.

There surely is no need to show the way for mourning such as this. Look above you and see the Christ stand, so pure, so chaste, so glorious in the light in which He arrays Himself as with a garment, and you will abhor yourself and repent in the dust. Look around you, and try to estimate the weight of a world's apostasy, the deluge of tears, the hurricane of sighs, that mount up to heaven. Ah, it's a sore world!

But the mourners are not content to shed tears only. *They hunger and thirst after righteousness* (Matt. 5:6). St. Augustine says that they hunger and thirst after the Righteous One— "Jesus Christ the Righteous." They were made for Him, and will never be satisfied until they attain to the fruition of all their hopes, to know Him, and the power of His resurrection and the fellowship of His sufferings (Phil. 3:10).

Without doubt such is their supreme desire, and included in this they hunger and thirst for the ultimate triumph of righteousness in their own hearts and in the world of people. Every moan of pain, every consciousness of failure, every temporary triumph of reactionary and destructive forces—elicits the more urgent and persistent prayer, "Thy Kingdom come" (Matt. 6:10). The personal coming of the Lord is desired not primarily because the Bride desires the

Bridegroom, but because the subject longs for the triumph of that Kingdom which is righteousness, joy, and peace in the Holy Spirit.

This aspiration is noble. Some hungers are ignoble, despicable, and base. But this one is shared in by God Himself, whose Spirit longs with an inexpressible desire to bring to an end the present condition of things in the vindication and manifestation of His sons and daughters. The angels, as they behold the evil and pain of our earth; the champion of the rights of people, who wrestles with the hydra-headed and protean evil of his age; the wronged womanhood of the harem and the street; the dumb Creation groaning and travailing with enormous and cruel wrongs—all join in this blessed hunger and thirst, the aspiration which amounts to a sure and certain hope that cannot be ashamed.

You need not be taught this, for you have often felt it. Amid the violet light of a dying summer's day, when soft and lovely music—songs without words—is filling the entranced and listening air, when some heroic stand for liberty is drowned and quenched in blood, when the white robes of the soul have been stained and polluted by some recent fall—then the soul hungers with an intolerable pain, and thirsts, as a wounded hart for water-brooks, that righteousness should set up its blessed and all-conquering reign.

CHAPTER THREE

THE ACTIVE SIDE OF THE BLESSED LIFE

(Matt. 5:7-12)

Let us now turn to the active side of the Blessed Life.

Blessed Are the Merciful

The merciful (Matt. 5:7) are not content with bearing wrong. They pity the wrongdoer, pity him with a great compassion, because they realize that a heart which inflicts wrong must itself be tortured by remorse, scourged with the whips of the Furies, and is certain to have an even more terrible awakening to shame and everlasting contempt. The merciful, therefore, go forth with a great longing to deliver the evildoer from himself.

It was thus that the Master felt when He bore the sins of His murderers in His own body on the tree, prayed for their forgiveness, and from His throne of glory sent the Spirit to turn the hearts of fathers to their children, and of the disobedient to the wisdom of the just.

The eyes of mercy are deep with compassionate glances, full of tears, the homes of prayer; the feet of mercy are soft in their tread, for they will not break the bruised reed, nor quench the smoldering spark in the dimly-burning flax; the voice of mercy is generous to the fallen, gentle to the weak, and gracious to the offender; from the heart of mercy soothing balm flows to the wounds of sinners, of sufferers, and of the world.

The only way in which you can become merciful is to remember how much mercy you need and have obtained. "Seeing," said the Apostle, that "we have obtained mercy, we faint not" (2 Cor. 4:1, ASV). Ah, think of the ten thousand talents that have been forgiven you, and you will not take your brother by the throat and demand the hundred pence in which he is a defaulter (Matt. 18:23-28). Have you forgotten the moment when you heard your Lord say, "Your sins, which were many, are forgiven"? and are you going to resent the approach of a sinful soul, which loathes the miserable past and longs to be emancipated from the burden of unforgiven sin? Remember your own exceeding bitter cry which God has recorded in His book: "Have mercy upon me, O God, according to Thy loving-kindness; according unto the multitude of Thy tender mercies" (Ps. 51:1).

Blessed Are the Pure in Heart

The divinely merciful become, in the very nature of things, *the pure of heart* (Matt. 5:8). They have come to estimate by their own inner experiences, and by the long effort which the inveterate sin of others has demanded, how terrible and horrible a thing sin is. The mother who has nursed one of her children through some loathsome and painful disease is filled with horror at it, and will take extravagant precautions to ward off the least germ or microbe that menaces her home. Only those who have been forgiven again and again, and who have forgiven, are quick to discern the first symptom of impurity, and to turn from it with shuddering horror. Yes, and to know what sin costs to those that have to deliver the sinner is such a revelation of the bitter suffering of the Redeemer, that, in view of what impurity costs Him, the soul flees from every taint of uncleanness, lest it should add one pang more to that heart which is already pierced through with many sorrows.

The way to purity is by love. If you would be pure, love Christ best of all, and love sinful people with a great pity, and love shall be in you like a fire. It is said that, when Adam and Eve were created and lived in Eden, they needed no garment of any kind, because their native innocence emitted rays of light which enswathed their persons as an atmosphere. As much may be said of love, for where it fills the heart it sheds forth light and fire, which proceed from the very center of our being, as the fire of God in the midst of the burning bush.

Blessed Are the Peacemakers

The pure in heart are naturally *the peacemakers* (Matt. 5:9), because they cannot rest satisfied that the world of people should remain alienated from the life and holiness of God. They become, therefore, messengers of peace and benediction, seeking to reconcile between God and people, or between different people, which is a most needful work if ever the wrongs of time are to be righted, and earth become the home of love.

The way to this is to ask God to tell you what work He is doing in the world, and whether you may be permitted to help Him. He will tell you that, having laid the foundations of peace in the Cross, He is going on to reconcile all things to Himself, whether they be in heaven, or on earth, or under the earth; and if you would have fellowship with Him, you must set yourself to deal with all that breaks peace in yourself and in others.

Often in their prayers God's servants ask Him to *help* them. Without doubt the phrase can be abundantly justified; but does it not suggest that God is to shape His activities to the mold of *our* schemes, and accompany *us* along *our* chosen path? Is it not better to realize that all the burden and responsibility rest upon Him who is mighty; and that all working, whether to will or do, must emanate from Him as the Fountain, and pass through us as the channel—submerging us as it passes forth to its blessed and victorious end?

Preeminently God is entitled "the God of Peace." He is ever engaged in healing the wounds and reconciling the enmities of the world. As nature covers the battlefield with golden harvests, so does God seek to undo the results of feud and strife, and lay foundations of justice for the temple of peace. Blessed indeed are they whom He associates with Himself in such pacific ministries.

Blessed Are Those Persecuted
for Righteousness' Sake

But all such become *persecuted* and hated (Matt. 5:10). It cannot be otherwise, apparently, in such a world as this. To have fellowship with the Lamb we must have fellowship in His rejection and suffering. The servant is not above his Lord, and therefore the Master said sadly: "Ye shall indeed drink of My cup, and be baptized with the baptism that I am baptized with" (Matt. 20:23).

It is impossible to follow the Lord closely, and not be spattered by the mud that was cast at Him. Indeed, to miss it may fill us with questionings. The soldier who follows the colonel through the thick of the fight will almost certainly have some scar to carry to his afteryears. We must see to it that all the evil is said against us *falsely* (Matt. 5:11), and that we are reproached for the name of Christ.

Rejoice and Be Glad

Is this your experience? Be of good cheer. You are on the track bedewed by the tears and blood of the martyrs of Jesus, and as they overcame, so shall you. Be faithful unto death, and He shall give you a crown of life (Matt. 5:12). But through all you shall have a secret joy, a secret supply of strength, and a sweet intimacy with Him who before Pontius Pilate witnessed the good confession.

It should be noticed that these Beatitudes run in a parallel line with 1 Corinthians 13, and show what Love can be and do.

Poverty in spirit is Love in her chosen garb of humility, for she vaunteth not herself, and is not puffed up. Meekness is Love in the presence of wrong. Mourning is Love in tears. Hunger is Love's appetite. Mercy is Love on her errands of beneficence. Purity is Love on fire. Peacemaking is Love's effort to adjust the wrong of the world. Persecution is Love's requital at the hands of those whom she would help. And Love is all this, intensely, perennially, constantly, because she cannot help it. Character has been defined as what a person is in the dark; and Love is all this, not for fee or reward, not for notoriety or advertisement, but because she cannot be other. To be this is to be herself.

But who is sufficient for these things? How can they be originated and perpetuated? What is their nutriment and support? There is but one reply. The Holy Spirit must come upon you and overshadow you; Christ must be formed in you; Heaven must descend to you before it can shine out from you.

It has been said that there is neither Cross nor Pentecost in the Sermon on the Mount, but surely they are implied. A broad, much-trodden road foretells the great City whither it leads, and these wonderful chapters inevitably conduct to Calvary and the Upper Room.

Let a person seek to attain to Christ's ideal, and he will discover the infinite disparity between its crystal heights and his ineffectual efforts to clamber to their majestic crest; he will need the propitiation and cleansing of the Blood of the Cross; he will confess to the weakness and impotence of the Flesh; he will lie at the feet of the Crucified as one dead, until the life of His resurrection enters to infill, indwell, and empower.

There is no hope of our being able to realize this exquisite portraiture by imitation or even by mediation. No; He who originally conceived this ideal, who Himself lived it, must incarnate Himself within us by the Holy Spirit, that He may reproduce in and through us that which He has inspired us to desire. He must give us what He commands; He must be in us what He prescribes.

CHAPTER FOUR

SILENT INFLUENCE

(Matt. 5:13)

Being is doing. Our greatest work for God and man is to be. The influence of a holy life is our greatest contribution to the salvation and blessing of the world. Though you cannot preach, or teach, or even if you cannot engage in some other sphere of Christian service, do not be greatly moved, if only you can live the life of God among people. Our Lord for thirty years was content to live an absolutely holy life, as the Lamb of God without blemish and without spot; and His supreme work in the world was not only to give His life as a ransom, but to live His life that He might leave us an example that we should follow in His steps (1 Peter 2:21).

Too many Christians seem to suppose that the main object of life is to engage in a sphere of direct service, while they leave their personal character to take care of itself, and to develop almost haphazardly; whereas our main thought and care should be that Christ should be formed in us, and be revealed in every look and gesture, every word and act. Out of that will come naturally, inevitably, and blessedly, our direct Christian service. The best work is that which arises out of the simplicity and beauty of our witness for truth and love.

We must, of course, guard against extremes. On the one

hand, we may attempt so much service as to neglect that inner culture which is priceless in its effect on service, and our personal inconsistencies will neutralize the effect of our Christian activities. On the other hand, we may sincerely believe that we are cultivating our character, when, in fact, we are sinking into a dreamy lethargy, from which we need to be aroused by the trumpet call of duty to a dying world. We are apt to forget that the development of the inner life is not perfect, unless it issues in such going about doing good (Acts 10:38), as was the flower and fruit of our Saviour's thirty years.

Persecution of the Lord's Followers

Though Persecuted. Our Lord had been describing the reception which the type of character that He had come to implant would certainly encounter. Instead of attracting people by its heavenly beauty, it would certainly repel them. Instead of commendation and welcome, it would arouse dislike and rebuff. The great world of people would not appreciate the poor in spirit, the mourner, the meek and merciful, the pure in heart, or maker of peace—but would reproach, and persecute, and say all manner of evil falsely. But, notwithstanding all, He insisted that they should continue to bless the world by the silent and gracious influence of holy lives. Reviled, they must bless; persecuted, they must endure; defamed, they must entreat; threatened with death, they must still be as salt to their persecutors, and as light to their defamers.

However people receive our testimony, whatever they may say and do against us, notwithstanding the unreasonableness of their dislike, we must continue to be what our Lord would have us be, nay, we must *let* Him who is within us shine forth through us, so that some people may be compelled to admit that the unearthly beauty of our lives is a supreme proof of the divinity and glory of our religion.

You ask what is the good of being good. Your detractors and oppressors vaunt themselves over you, take every advantage of your quiet, unresisting gentleness, and misinterpret your self-restraint. It would almost appear that they are driven to greater extremes of wickedness because of the provocation of your goodness. The soldiers of the Roman governor probably never mocked one of their ordinary victims as they did the holy, unresisting Saviour. A gentle and loving wife will sometimes extract the most malignant and bitter hatred of her husband, such as he would show to no other. But you do not know if your behavior is beginning to thaw that iron-frozen soil, or how often and deeply compunction is at work, or how nearly the hatred of your oppressor is being overcome by love. The spring warmth may seem to fall on the frozen masses of snow and ice in vain, but every hour of sunshine is sapping the reign of the ice-king, and hastening the inevitable breakup of his supremacy.

That workingman who has borne the insults of his shopmates for Christ may presently have the ringleader come to beg his pardon, and with tears in his eyes ask him to pray for him. That oppressed wife may have the pleasure of leading her penitent husband to the cross. That sister, who has borne contumely and reproach with unswerving gentleness, may be won by her loving sister. Be of good cheer, your sufferings will eventually have their most blessed result in overcoming evil by good. Remember, the Apostle speaks of "the Kingdom and patience of Jesus" (Rev. 1:9), which means that patient suffering ultimately secures a blessed supremacy, a royalty, an overmastery of hardness and unkindness by gentleness, truth, and love.

When the Forth Bridge was being built, the workmen came to a crucial point, where two of the most important iron girders refused by some inches to come together for the bolts to be driven through—a process which was absolutely essential to their union and the stability of the whole bridge. Every mechanical method to bring them together was tried, to no avail. Finally, in despair, all further efforts were abandoned for the night. It was summer weather, and the sunshine of the following morning was very hot, so much so that the great masses of metal expanded beneath the genial rays, and the results were achieved by the silent touch of the sun which had defied the utmost efforts of force. So in human life. Consistency of character, purity, gentleness, sweetness, such holy living as issues from the qualities which our Lord has enumerated, will avail when the keepers of the house shall tremble, and the strong men will bow themselves (Ec. 12:3)..

Condition of the World

The Lord knew well the *condition of the world.* To His holy and unerring judgment it was a carcass slowly rotting to putrefaction, and sorely needing some influence to stay its corruption. There was never an epoch in the world's history fuller of dazzling genius than that in which He was born. Some of the most brilliant names of history were shining still in the midnight sky when the bright and morning star arose over Bethlehem. But the grossness of the age was unparalleled and indescribable. The allusions made to it in the Epistles are sufficiently terrible, but the whole truth is only revealed in classic literature itself, which survives to show that the earth was corrupt before God, and that every imagination of the thoughts of people's hearts was only evil continually (Gen. 6:5).

In our Lord's eyes, also—to refer to the other metaphor—the world lay under the power of thick darkness. In its wisdom it knew not God. Professing themselves wise, men had become fools. The god of this world had blinded the eyes of those who believed not, and they groped in the noontide as in the murky midnight. Such has been, is, and will be, the condition of people without the Gospel. The history of the human family is always repeating itself. We cannot be surprised either at the description given by missionaries of the awful condition of heathen countries, or at the outbreaks of lawlessness and crime in nations which are only nominally Christian. Our inventions, organizations, and boasted civilization may affect the exterior of our society, but if it were not for the presence of the Church of the Lord Jesus, and the witness borne by the lives and words of her members, there would be nothing to save it from the pit of corruption, which has swallowed up every great nation that has risen to lead the race.

Men rage against " Exeter Hall," and revile what is called "the Nonconformist Conscience," as they did against the Puritans in bygone centuries, not realizing that they who rage evince the antagonism of corruption to the salt, and of darkness to the light, and that the very existence of our society is more largely due than they suppose to the very elements they so much dislike.

You Are the Earth's Salt

Salt (Matt. 5:13). Our consistent holy living will act as an antiseptic to arrest the corruption around us. It is said that the presence of a little child, with its blue-eyed simplicity and purity, has often arrested the commission of dark crimes; and as much should be said of the influence of our own daily living. A sudden silence should fall on certain kinds of conversation when we enter the room. This or the other form of worldly amusement, which has entered professedly Christian homes, should be felt out of place when we are staying there. And right through the society in which we move there should be a consciousness that there is an incongruity between our character and all that savors of impurity, falsehood, and selfishness.

We do not want to impose a sense of restraint and gloom on social gatherings when we enter. Our presence should be an incentive to the merriment of the children, the cheer of the depressed, the gladness of young and old. Flowers should burst into beauty at our steps, songs should overflow in our paths, and innocent laughter should be our accompaniment. The mountains and the hills should break forth before us into singing, and all the trees of the field should clap their hands. Instead of the thorn should come up the fir tree, and instead of the briar the myrtle tree (Isa. 55:13). But to all that is unseemly and unworthy our presence should act as an antiseptic.

A young boy, fresh from his mother's teaching and prayers, was plunged suddenly into a large lawyer's office, to serve as an apprentice. At first he was bewildered by his strange surroundings, then the crimson mantled his cheek, and tears brimmed in his eyes. "What's the matter with you, youngster?" said a coarse voice. "Do you want to go back to your mother's apron strings?"

"No," was the reply, "but we never said such things in my mother's home as you say here."

The answer elicited a burst of laughter, but the head of the office said: "Gentlemen, this lad is right, and as long as he stays with us I must request that you modify your speech." And from that moment the whole tone of that office was altered. The lad's presence acted as salt.

We may easily lose our savor. Salt left in contact with a damp soil ceases to be salty, and is good for nothing but to be trodden underfoot. It is neither fit for the ground nor the dunghill. Lot lost his savor. Sodom went on its way, regardless of his presence in its midst. The Seven Churches of Asia lost their savor, and, with those of Northern Africa, were trodden down by the Muslims. Nothing is so useless and worthless as an inconsistent and powerless Christian (Ezek. 15:3-5). Oh, break your heart if sin is as shameless and reckless in your presence as in your absence! What have you done to forfeit the power you should exert? Repent, and do the first works! Yea, ask the Lord Jesus to infuse into you His own strong, sweet, pure nature, before whom the demons were driven forth, and by whose presence, through His Church in the world, an arrest has been placed on many of those grosser forms of sin which disgraced the world of His time, and still hold sway in countries where His name is not known.

CHAPTER FIVE

LIGHTED TO SHINE

(Matt. 5:14-16)

"Not that Light" (John 1:8). No, not even John the Baptist was that. There is only one true Light, "which lighteth every man that cometh into the world" (John 1:9), even He who is the Life of men. We are lights; He is "that Light." We are stars that have no original glory, and if one differs from another in the radiance which he sheds forth, it is only insofar as he reflects more fully the luster of that uncreated Sun. Centuries ago that Sun shone in this world, without a dimming cloud between His glory and the world of mankind, except the veil of His flesh; but so far as the world was concerned there was sunset, while it was yet noon, on Calvary, and we have been summoned to take up His mission and shine as stars in the midnight sky, or as candles in the darkened home, until the first beams of the eternal morning break on the Alpine summits of time, white with the snows of millenniums.

You Are the Earth's Light

It is interesting to apply the analogy between the Disciples of Christ and candles or lamps. "The spirit of man is the candle of the Lord" (Prov. 20:27). By nature we are like so many unlighted candles. As a candle is adapted to catch the light, but stands dark and cold until its wick is ignited, so have our natures been made to burn and shine with the nature of God, but they are unable to produce light of themselves, and remain cold and dark until kindled from the eternal Nature of Him who is Light, for "in Him is no darkness at all" (1 John 1:5). It matters little what the nature of the candlestick may be. In your case it may be of gold, silver, or china. It may be exquisitely made, or of the commonest possible manufacture. The most ornate candlestick is incapable of producing the Light, and will be set aside in favor of the commonest dip stuck on the end of a piece of wood if only that has caught the precious Light of which *the other* is destitute. The Pharisees and Scribes of our Lord's time were like handsome candelabra, which gave no ray of light to the thick darkness of their age; while His disciples, humble fishermen, shone with a light which has irradiated all succeeding time.

"Men light a candle" (Matt. 5:15). They place the wick against some burning point of light, or they strike a match, or in our days turn a switch, and immediately there is a glow of light *which abashes darkness, and enables the housewife to find her lost piece of silver.* O soul, have you been lighted? Have you come in contact with Christ, or with one of His servants in whom His nature has shown, or with His Word, which may be compared to a box of matches, because all the potentiality of fire and light slumbers until called into requisition? If not, stand expectant and eager; cry to Him, "Light me, O Light of Life, and let my nature henceforth have no other purpose than to shine on earth as Thou shinest in the Eternal Glory, emitting a radiance of the same nature and yielding the same prism as Thine own."

"The Life was Light" (John 1:4). Notice those words. Christ was the Light of men, not primarily because He wrought miracles and spoke wonderful words, but because He lived! He was the Light of Nazareth, because He lived within the circumference of its hills for thirty silent years. Galilee of the Gentiles—"the people which sat in darkness" (Matt. 4:16)—saw a great Light, because "He came and dwelt in Capernaum, which is by the sea" (Matt. 4:13, ASV). The country of the Jews was illumined because He "went about

doing good, and healing all that were oppressed" (Acts 10:38). The silent influence of that Life which unfolded itself in the loveliness of perfect deeds has stolen over the world like dawn over the sky; and if the Lord had never spoken a word, the testimony of His life for God and Truth and Love would have been the most remarkable episode in human annals.

It must be so with us; we shine by what we are. We shine as there is less of the wick of *our own* nature, and more of the flame of *His*. We shine when we are unselfish, when we "do all things without murmurings and questionings"; when we are "blameless and harmless children of God without blemish" (Phil. 2:14-15, ASV). Though you were never to speak a word you might still fulfill the greatest mission and ministry of your life, if only you would live as Christ lived.

"He was a burning and a shining light" (John 5:35). The Baptist shone because he burned. His light cost him his life. On one occasion he said, "I must decrease" (John 3:30); probably his ministry lasted only a few months. The light he gave was so brilliant that it exhausted him prematurely. There can be no true shining without burning. The light that cost you nothing is hardly worth the giving. You ought to be burning down to the socket, as you spend and are spent for others. Your zeal for God's house should burn you up.

Burning also stands for heat. John was fervent, intense, passionate in his devotion. His was an ardent nature, that loved as few people love. The love that others give to wife and child and friend, in his case was expended on his Lord. Mary did not more certainly break an alabaster box on the head and feet of Jesus, than he the rich perfume of his lovely nature.

See that there is fervor, ardor, passion, and the fire of a burning heart behind your testimony for the Saviour. Socrates gave light; he shone, but did not burn. Wesley gave light, but he burned; and it is hardly possible to read a page of his sermons without being warmed at the fire of his intense nature. What shall we say of the Great Apostle whose nature was ignited on the road to Damascus, and who said that whether he seemed beside himself or sober, he was mastered by one passion, and constrained by the love of Christ?

The Candle and the Bushel

It would be absurd to take the trouble to light a lamp, and then obscure its rays by placing it beneath a corn measure. The purpose of ignition would be counteracted and frustrated if any inmate of the house were to cover the light. But how many of God's children have placed bushels on the light of their daily testimony for God? The bushel of uncharitable speech! The bushel of peevish and murmuring complaint! The bushel of an unforgiving spirit! The bushel of some conspicuous failing! Any of these is sufficient to counteract the entire effect of our testimony. On one occasion, when a mother was remonstrating with her grown-up son for his not having become a Christian, he replied, "Mother, you have always seemed so afraid of God. Whenever anything has gone wrong in your life, you have been so put out, so fearful about the future, that you have made us think that we can get on as well without religion as with it." Is not this a specimen case of the bushels which cover our lights? Whenever you hear someone say, "He is a very good man, but—;" or "She is a very good woman, only—," you may be sure that there is some bushel in the life which is forbidding the outshining of the Life.

Notice what the Master says. *"Let* your light . . . shine" (Matt. 5:16). It is not for you to ignite the flame, to supply the oil, or trim the wick; your simple duty is to guard against anything that may obstruct the outshining of the Life of God from your soul. If only you see to it that everything that might hinder the effect of your testimony and mar your influence is put away, Christ will see to it that your light shall effect the full measure of His purpose. Let those words ring in your heart, *"Let* your light . . . shine." Allow it to shine; guard against everything which would prevent its shining.

In contrast with the bushel is the stand or *candlestick*, not under the bushel, but on the stand. What is your stand? Is it not your station in society, your position in your home, the sphere of your influence, your position in that business house, factory, or workshop?

With infinite care and forethought, God has chosen the very place in which you can do your best work for the world. You may be lonely, but you have no more right to complain than the lamp has, which has been placed in a niche to illumine a dark landing or a flight of dangerous stone steps. The Master of the house may have put you in a very small corner, and on a very humble stand; but it is enough if it is His blessed will. Someday He will pass by, and you shall light His steps as He goes forth to seek and save that which is lost; or you shall turn on some great light that shall shine like a beacon over a storm-swept ocean. Thus the obscure Andrew was the means of igniting his brother Peter when he brought him to Jesus.

What a good thing it is when a Christian takes his bushel off his light, turns the bushel upside down, and places the light on it! Suppose, for instance, a person's bushel has been the love of strong drink. Let him conquer it, and put it under his feet; let him became an apostle of total abstinence; let him win other drink-cursed lives. Then that which had threatened to extinguish his influence will be the means of extending it, for others who have been cursed as he has been will naturally turn to him for help. It is a blessed thing when the fire of Divine Love kindles the bushels themselves, destroying them and making a conflagration which compels people to turn from the power of darkness toward its attractive glow.

The Motive for Service

Never forget that the one object in Holy Living is not to convince people, but to "glorify your Father which is in Heaven" (Matt. 5:16). If you live with your thoughts directed toward people, even though your motive is one of pure beneficence on their behalf, you will have less influence upon them than you will exert if your life is altogether Godward, and your one aim be that He may be glorified.

The glory of the Father was the one motive that occupied the mind of our Lord from the hour when at age twelve He said, "I must be about My Father's business" (Luke 2:49), to that other when He stood under the shadow of His Cross, and said: "I have glorified Thee on the earth" (John 17:4; see also John 14:13; 15:8). So live, speak, and love, that God may be glorified, and count your life a failure unless people turn from you to Him. It is not enough for your light to shine; it must *so* shine. Any shining which does not make people glorify God is deficient. Good it may be, but it is not the best. Your light must be so managed that people do not talk about *you*, but about *Him* who has made you what you are.

"Whether therefore ye eat, or drink, or whatsoever ye do, do all to the glory of God" (1 Cor. 10:31).

The Fuel Supply

God will supply the lamp with oil. After all, we are but wicks, to the edge of which, as upon a ladder, the oil climbs from the cistern. Who could see to read or work by the burning of a wick? No; it is *the oil* that burns on the wick, while the wick slowly chars, as it yields itself to mediate between the fire on the one hand and the oil on the other. Keep on burning, O Christian soul! God will never fail you, however long your life may be, and however dark the night! God will supply you with the oil that flows from the two olive trees that set forth Christ's dual work as Priest and King (Lev. 24:1-4; Zech. 4:1-3).

It is the constant fear of some Christian workers that they will never hold out. But that should not be their care. Christ ever lives, Christ ever loves, and Christ is ever and all-sufficient. Draw upon Him; let all your fresh springs be in Him; let Him be what God meant Him to be—"wisdom . . . righteousness . . . sanctification, and redemption" (1 Cor. 1:30).

The Necessary Trimming

God will certainly have to trim your light. He will leave this sacred business to no other hand than His own; and He reserves for it "snuffers . . . of pure gold" (1 Kings 7:50).

Very often one's soul dreads the application of His providences that seems to threaten it with extinguishment. It turns out, however, that the love of God was only cutting away something which was hindering our uprightness, that the true flame might break out more completely. There may be limitation on the area of illumination, but there will be marked increase in the intensity of the radiance. The limitation of Paul's imprisonment meant the lasting power of his Epistles. The snuffers of Bedford Jail produced *Pilgrim's Progress*.

Ask for a radiant life, and trust God to take the best means possible in accomplishing an abundant answer to your request.

CHAPTER SIX

CHRIST, THE COMPLETEMENT OF HUMAN LIFE

(Matt. 5:17-20)

The first question that a historian asks of a new teacher is, "What is your relation to the past? What have you to say of the great prophets and teachers, at whose feet for generations our forefathers have sat?"

To that question the reply has often been, "My mission is to destroy; you have been misled; the path by which former generations have traveled is by no means the easiest or best. I have come to suggest that we wipe the slate, that we obliterate the past, that we begin by laying new foundations on which to construct a larger and more commodious erection."

This is the creed of the revolutionary. In the French Revolution, Robespierre and his confederates went so far as to obliterate our weekly division of time, insisting that a week should consist of ten rather than seven days. New names were affixed to the days, to the streets, and to the officials of the State. But it was not thus that Christ inaugurated His work. He answered the *thoughts* of His age, saying, "Think not that I am come to destroy." Every "jot and tittle" of the ancient code was dear to Him. Jesus was no iconoclast. Radical though He was in going to the very roots of things, He was not a revolutionary.

As the noon fulfills the dawn, as summer fulfills the spring, as manhood fulfills childhood, as a great artist fulfills the struggling ideal of the generality of people in a poem, statue, or sonata, so does Jesus Christ gather up the highest ideals inspired by God's Spirit in people's hearts or engraven by His hand on tablets of stone. Wherever there is suggestion of eternal truth He realizes it, and shows people the steps by which they may climb to its lofty level.

A Purposeful Destruction

Of course, there was a measure of destruction. When the Epistle of the Hebrews was written the institutions of the Old Covenant were becoming old, waxing aged, and were nigh unto vanishing away (Heb. 8:13). But the destruction was only part of the natural process through which the ideal of the ancient Scriptures was being fulfilled. It was not a destruction which left no trace, as when a fire destroys an artist's studio, burning sketch and picture, the plaster cast and the finished statue—but the destruction of the less perfect form in face of the finished and completed design. Thus the rough sketch is superseded by the finished painting, the bud by the flower, the toys and the lesson books of childhood by the interests of the mature man. The emblems of kindergarten fulfill their work in a child's mind by giving it conceptions of shape and form, and some rudimentary knowledge. They are then cast aside; but the conceptions that they helped to form are the permanent possession of the nature which thus made its first trials on the tiny lake before it launched out upon the mighty ocean with its boundless horizon.

The Aaronic Priesthood was destroyed that it might be fulfilled in the one unchangeable priesthood of the Son of God. The altars on which ten thousand victims had been consumed were destroyed, and their ashes poured out upon the ground, because they were fulfilled in that one Altar on which the supreme Propitiation was made. The Temple was destroyed, because the Shekinah of God's Presence had gone forth to fulfill that temple which is composed of saved souls, and of which the Apostle says that "the building fitly framed together groweth unto an holy temple in the Lord" (Eph. 2:21). The whole system of ceremonial observance, with which Leviticus is full, has been destroyed, because love has come to be the inner principle of the Christian heart, and "Love is the fulfilling of the Law."

A Purposeful Fulfillment

Under the term *"Law and Prophets"* our Lord includes, by a familiar Jewish abbreviation, the entire range of the Old Testament (Matt. 7:12; 22:40; Luke 16:16; 24:44; Acts 13:15). It is probable that He never possessed a copy of the Old Testament Scriptures for His own private use. The only Bible that was within His reach was that which was kept in the synagogue; but on His retentive memory and heart as a Child, Mary in the home, and the old Rabbi in the school of the synagogue, and, above all, the Spirit of Inspiration Himself, had deeply written the whole text of Sacred Writ. It was thus that He knew the Scriptures, though He had never learned in the schools of the metropolis.

Nothing could exceed our Lord's reverence for the Scriptures. He quotes or refers to them about 400 times. With these He parried the temptations of the wilderness; met and foiled the criticisms of Pharisee and Scribe; and consoled His own heart when it was fainting amid the shadows of Calvary. Everything that the Psalmist had said of the Law and Testimonies of God was literally appropriated by Jesus. They were sweet as honey to His taste, "yea . . . sweeter . . . .than honey and the honeycomb" (Ps. 19:10). In them He found the germ of the Messianic ideal, which He realized in altogether unexpected ways, and to fulfill which was His one eager purpose. It is with profound significance that we are told that on the Cross He knew that "all things" had been "finished" with the exception of the one Scripture, which told how the rejected hind of the morning should be parched with thirst and receive at the hand of its foes, not water, but vinegar; then "that the Scripture might be accomplished," He said, "I thirst" (John 19:28, ASV).

From first to last, the life of our Lord was the fulfillment in spirit and letter of the ancient ritual. As the Son of the Law, He obeyed the initial rite of Judaism on the eighth day after birth, and there was no item of the Law, even to dots of the *i*'s or the crossing of the *t*'s which he omitted or slurred. He "died for our sins according to the Scriptures, and . . . He rose again the third day according to the Scriptures" (1 Cor. 15:3-4). What could only be partially true of His Apostle was literally true of the Lord, as "touching the righteousness which is in the Law," He was found "blameless" (Phil. 3:6).

Our Lord fulfilled the ceremonial Law (Luke 2:21-22, 27; Gal. 4:4), and fulfilled the moral Law, since He was "Jesus Christ the Righteous" (1 John 2:1); He honored the Law by His obedience "even to death," atoning for its breach and violation by mankind, and giving through His unknown sufferings an answer to its just dues and demands, such as could not have been afforded though the whole race had been fined to the uttermost farthing of penal consequences. His fulfillment, therefore, was not for Himself alone, but as the second Adam, the representative Man, and for us all.

The Law and Christ's Love

"The Law made nothing perfect" (Heb. 7:19), because it dealt so largely with particular instances and external observances, and people sought to satisfy it by an obedience which consisted almost wholly in "meats and drinks. . . and carnal ordinances" (Heb. 9:10), imposed until the time of reformation. A servant in a home who has been carefully trained may fulfill all the outward demands of household work; but how different is the service which is compelled by an outward rule, and compensated for by the specified wage, from the service which the wife and mother gives, inspired by a love which feeds upon the sacrifices it makes! The Law could not produce perfect people, because it did not as yet deal with the principle of the self-life which vitiates our best obedience. Indeed, the ancient ritual, in most cases, even developed the self-principle, as in the case of the Pharisees, because the accumulation of outward obedience was deemed to produce a large amount of merit, and therefore to produce a higher place in the sight of God.

Our Lord, on the other hand, came to teach that love would fulfill all demands of the Law and the Prophets, *and more.* He taught that to love one's neighbor would be the fulfillment of the Law, and that obedience to every Commandment was summed up in one word, "Thou shalt love." In Christ's teaching the whole Law was fulfilled in this one word, "Thou shalt love" (Rom. 8:8-10; Gal. 5:14).

"Do we then make void the Law through faith? (Rom. 3:31) "No; since faith is capacity for God, it receives out of His fullness the baptism of perfect love. More and more as we love "we establish the Law" (Rom. 3:31). In proportion as we walk after the Spirit of Love the requirement of the Law is "fulfilled in us" (Rom. 8:4). Thus Christ, in shedding His love "abroad in our hearts" (Rom. 5:5) becomes "the end of the Law for righteousness" to all who believe (Rom. 10:4), and we present before God a reverence for the ancient Scriptures, and a fulfillment of their precepts, which are produced in our deepest nature by the Spirit of Love.

Is your soul enamored with the love of some great ideal? And is it the complaint of your life that it has been too high for you to attain? Are you lying at the foot of the cliff, bruised and mangled by repeated failure? Are you almost in despair? Be of good cheer, Christ has come "not to destroy, but to fulfill," to take each yearning purpose and conduct it to maturity, to show how every desire for goodness may be realized, how the crescent of promise may become the full orb of fulfillment, and to accomplish in you and for you, here and hereafter, every "jot and tittle" of the Divine demands.

CHAPTER SEVEN

LOVE AGAINST ANGER

(Matt. 5:21-26)

They of "old time," the philosophers and legislators of mankind, saw that murderous anger strikes at the very existence of the human family, and must be arrested. They therefore prohibited it, and accompanied their prohibition by a threat of condemnation before their high courts. "Whosoever shall kill," they said, "shall be in danger of the judgment" (Matt. 5:21).

But neither prohibition nor threatening availed. The dams they built were all too weak to resist the tides of hatred and revenge that swept against their frail resistance. People agreed that those laws were good. In their saner moments they acquiesced and assisted. But when the storm arose within they were swept headlong from the thought to the wish, from the wish to the fully-formed purpose, from purpose to word, and from word to act.

Then the Love of God incarnate stood among people. His legislation began further back, in the genesis of sin. He does not deal with the act of murder, but sees, first, the explosion of wrath in speech—*Fool*; then behind this to the feeling of dislike—*Vain* fellow; and behind this again the anger of the heart, concealed from all eyes but His. In His judgment chamber that anger is as evil as murder is at the bar of man. He metes out to it the same condemnation that human society allots to the murderer. He says that everyone who is angry with his brother is in danger of the judgment court, constituted to deal with murder. Jesus does not say, "Thou shalt not kill," because He deals instead with the springs of will, thought, and action, creating a clean heart, renewing a right spirit, removing the evil disposition out of which murder springs. What need to tell someone that he must not kill his brother, when he has been led to love that person as himself?

Defeated by Anger

Our Lord refers to two tribunals of the Jewish commonwealth—the local magistrate's court, which had the power of life and death, and inflicted death by beheading; and the Sanhedrin, or final Court of Appeal, in Jerusalem, whose sentence of death was executed by stoning. There was a fate considered more terrible than either, when the body of a criminal was cast forth as refuse into the Valley of Gehenna, here described as "hell fire" (Matt. 5:22) because fires were always burning in its forbidding precincts to destroy the rubbish and garbage that would have poisoned the city's health. Where there is no system of drainage, as in Eastern cities, the pariah dog, the fire, and the worm are indispensable.

In Christ's Kingdom unwarrantable anger would be liable to the lower court, the anger that vented itself in slighting and contemptuous phrase to the higher, and the anger that exploded in vehement and passionate epithets would lead to the fate of a castaway. Jesus did not go beyond this, because the crime of murder would be impossible to those in whose hearts the first sparks had been judged and condemned. In the legislation of Christ, someone who hates his brother is a murderer, and any that allow hate to smolder, unchecked and unrepented of, are guilty of a capital offence against His laws, and forfeit all the rights and privileges of His Kingdom, in the same way that murder causes the murderer to forfeit all the rights and privileges of the nation to which he belongs.

These are solemn words. They are quick and powerful, and sharper than any two-edged sword (Heb. 4:12). They pierce to the dividing asunder of soul and spirit, and criticize the thoughts and intents of the heart. They make us look up at this humblest and meekest of men speaking with such authority, as He sets Himself above the level of the men of old time, with His majestic "I say unto you" (Matt. 5:22), and lo—His eyes are as a flame of fire!

O, human soul, He looks into you and through you. Are you angry with your brother with the heat of a selfish and unjustifiable anger? If so, you have already been summoned to Christ's bar! Are you cherishing bitter contempt toward him? If so, you have been already condemned to suffer the death of the blasphemer, for you are cursing one made in the image of God! Are you flaming with vehement wrath, like a burning furnace? If so, you are already in the hell of fire; it needs not that you should wait for dissolution of soul and body. The flames of hell have already fastened on you. Your sin is automatic in the penal suffering it inflicts. Thus from our hearts we come to justify Christ, and realize that He is greater than the greatest people of all time.

Dealing with Anger

He goes deeper still, and shows how we may deal with the first motions of our spirit against an ill feeling which, after long smoldering, breaks out into so great a holocaust.

So often are we angry with people whom we have wronged; there is, therefore, no better way of saving us from explosions of anger than by undoing the wrong so soon as we become conscious of it in the clear light of God's presence. For this reason our Lord bids us find the person whom we have wronged, and make amends.

Again, when we review the past hours in the twilight of any ordinary day, we often become aware that, though we have not allowed our ill feeling to have its way, yet we have given some manifestation of it in a coldness of manner or change in behavior which must have been noticed by our former friend, and have rankled deeply in his mind. The symptom of our altered feeling toward him may have been very slight, but quite sufficient to indicate, like the storm signal on the coast, that there has been a depression in the atmosphere of our soul, and a storm is brewing. There is no more certain method of staying the progress of a tempest of anger than by at once becoming reconciled to the brother or sister over that one small detail in which our antagonism has revealed itself.

For each of these reasons, therefore, it is according to the deepest philosophy of the soul that our Lord bids us go to anyone who may justly have some cause of complaint against us, because of our manner, speech, or act.

Dissolving Anger

The altar, of which the Master speaks (Matt. 5:23), denotes some act of self-surrender to His adorable service which we are eager to make. Beside it stands the High Priest, waiting to consummate our gift, adding to it the merit of His intercession. The light of the Shekinah fire, which waits to consume the gift, is shining with intense brilliancy. All is prepared for the devout act of the soul which, constrained by the mercies of God, is about to present itself a holy, reasonable, and living sacrifice. Suddenly our great Melchizedek turns a searching light upon the hours which have recently passed. Every incident stands as clearly revealed as the objects in a landscape illumined by the lightning flash at midnight. And we hear His voice saying solemnly and searchingly, Has "thy brother . . . aught against thee?" (Matt. 5:23)

At first we shudder before the inquiry. We are conscious of some hidden wrong. The stiletto with which we struck at him was so sharp and slender that we assured ourselves against ourselves that the thrust must have escaped Christ's notice. But now we are aware that He, whose eyes carry the light with which they see, beheld it. We cannot deceive Him, but we evade His inquiry by enumerating the many causes of complaint that we have against the person who has been the subject of our Lord's question.

"He has not treated me as I had every right to expect. He has been ungrateful, ungracious, intolerant. He has not considered my interests. He has taken advantage of my goodwill. I never can get along with him; his temperament and mine are so different. Why did You give him to me as my brother? Had it been anyone else, I could have agreed. Outwardly I have tried to do my best. Can You wonder that I hide a grudge in my heart, and that almost involuntarily it betrays its presence? But, after all, the incident was a very slight one; no doubt he has forgotten it before now. He is accustomed to giving me ugly knocks; probably his skin is too thick to feel so slight an evidence of my unfriendliness."

Again, the searching voice enquires: Has "thy brother aught . . . against thee?"

"It depends, O Master," we reply, "in what court the case is tried. In any human court so slight a thing as that which stands revealed in this fierce light would be passed over as too trivial for notice. Before a jury of my friends, or even of my acquaintances, it would be admitted that I had not done anything so very wrong. It might be supposed that I was becoming morbid and introspective were I to take action on such a triviality."

Again, that clear, strong voice is heard saying: "We will not quibble. You know that your brother is suffering, and he is losing faith in your profession of religion, that he is being prejudiced against Me. Your parrying of My question is your condemnation. You know what you have done. In excusing, you accuse yourself. Leave your gift at the altar. Go first and be reconciled to him. Then return; I will await you. Though hours may pass, you will find Me here."

"May I not offer my gift now, and then find my brother? My heart is full of desire. I am eager to be an entire burnt offering to my God. Will not this fervor pass away, and leave me chilled?"

"Not so," the Master answers. "Your present gift will not be acceptable to God. The impetuous desire to make it is of the flesh, not of the Spirit. If it were of the Spirit there would be no doubt about its ultimate permanence. To obey is better than sacrifice, and to hearken than the fat of lambs (1 Sam 15:22). Be quick. The sky is darkening with night. The road that remains to be traversed by your brother, who has now become your adversary, is short. Agree with him quickly while you are in the way, lest by delay the quarrel between you and him becomes aggravated, and you find yourself in difficulties from which extrication will be impossible. Every moment of delay intensifies the sense of injustice, and makes more difficult your attempt at reconciliation."

"But he has wronged me, gracious Master. Is nothing to be said to him?"

"Not in the first place," is the reply. "It is necessary that you should retract your part, whatever it may be. Ask his forgiveness for that ruffled feeling, that unkind and harsh bearing, that icy reserve. Pay him any due that he may rightfully claim. Ask his forgiveness as you would ask God's, and your approach will bring a flood of repentant and protesting words, which will show that you have won your brother. But if these do not follow, and he receives your apology as his right, or without remark, still you have done your part, and there is nothing to be said against you further. I will deal with him—then come and offer your gift."

What music then is in that word *Come!* (Matt. 5:24) All heaven speaks in the invitation. Come, says the Master, and render yourself a living sacrifice, which is your reasonable service. Come and let Me make of you so much as is possible in your brief life. Come, for all things are ready.

And we discover this—that when we have acted as love should act, not because we *feel* the love, but because the Master bids us, and we simply obey, then the Love of God bursts up in our hearts like a hot geyser spring, and we find ourselves able to offer our gifts to God with an emotion of love that we could never have experienced otherwise.

This is the glory of our Lord's teaching, that when we do what is right, altogether apart from the emotion of pleasure or desire, we find ourselves glad to do it. In the right act there comes the right feeling, and in doing His will we are able to say, "I rejoice to do Thy will, O my God."

Try it. Be indifferent to emotion. Act. Then the emotion will burst out like the flowers that carpet the meadows in May. The birds will sing, the streams will flow, the flowers will appear, because by one act the reign of the Frost King is broken.

CHAPTER EIGHT

THE RULE OF THE EYE

(Matt. 5:27-30)

We have already seen that if a person permits his heart to be filled with anger that perpetually boils over or explodes in hard and contemptuous expressions he is excluded from the Kingdom of Heaven, and cast away as useless—the fire of Gehenna being a well-known expression for the rubbish heap. We are now led a step further, and are taught that impurity may have the same terrible effect, unless its earliest motions be sternly repressed. Indeed, Christ teaches that what is as natural as a right hand or eye, may, unless rigorously ruled, become the cause of a whole body being cast into Gehenna.

The outward and inward, the expression by the body and the passionate desire of the lower region of the soul (which we might call the animal soul), act and react on each other. The former influences the latter as the pouring of oil arouses a smothered flame. On the other hand, through the combination of desire and imagination, contriving together in the dark caverns of the soul, the body may become an instrument of deeds that make the pure stars blush.

The legislators of the old time laid it down that no member of the commonwealth should commit adultery, and enacted terrible penalties if their prohibition were trampled underfoot (Deut. 22:24); but the Divine Man, who reads the heart of people, goes back behind the deed to its early stages, legislates about the look that may inflame passion, and condemns the soul that does not instantly turn the eye from that which allures it, to the All-Holy, asking to be cleansed, not with tears only, but with blood, and pleading that the eye henceforth may be filmed with pity, melted into tenderness, and set on fire with the light of *His* eyes, that are described as being like a flame of fire.

The importance of the Regimen of the Eye is acknowledged in many places of Scripture: "When the woman saw that the tree was good for food, and that it was pleasant to the eyes" (Gen. 3:6). "Lot lifted up his eyes, and beheld all the plain . . . of Sodom" (Gen. 13:10). It was to David's straying glances that his great sin was due (2 Sam. 11:2). The Psalmist asked that his eyes may be turned away from beholding vanity (Ps. 119:37). Job made a covenant with his eyes (Job 31:1), and the Wise Man tells us not to look upon the wine when it is red, and gives its color in the cup (Prov. 23:31). Each passage enforces our Lord's words.

Thoughts and Intentions

The first step in the religious life is to detect right and wrong, not in the act, but in the thought and intention. If sin is arrested there, it is arrested in its earliest stage. If one's inward senses are exercised and trained to discern good and evil, and when one's soul not only discerns, but resists, there is no fear of that life being mastered by the tempter. The snake is killed in the egg; the microbe is destroyed before it can breed; the enemy is defeated before he can become ensconced within the city walls.

It is a remarkable fact to how small an extent many professing Christians practice this discernment between things that differ. They are quite willing to admit that the soul has senses, duplicated with those of the body; that it has eyes with which it may see God; ears by which it may hear the inner voice; the sense of touch, and even of smell, by which to distinguish between the wholesome and the corrupt, between the air of Paradise and the breath of the pit. But they have never learned to exercise them, to note and act upon their earliest suggestion (Heb. 5:14). This is the cause of infinite failure, and keeps such Christians in the stage of babyhood. They never become full grown, nor partake of the solid food of the Word (compare also 1 Cor. 3:1-2).

A curious illustration of this happened to me once. A Christian lady was very anxious that I should read a certain novel which had just come out and was attracting wide interest. She assured me that I should find much that I would approve of and enjoy. Acting on her advice, I took the book to beguile some leisure hours on the Atlantic, and sat down one afternoon on my deck chair to enjoy it. When, however, I reached page 50, I flung it over into the ocean, as I thought its contents would injure the fishes less than myself. If I had continued to read that story I would have been playing with fire.

What made the difference between that Christian lady and myself? Was it not that my inner senses were more sensitive than hers, and able to discern the evil of the book, which she would have unwittingly permitted to poison and contaminate her entire nature? Some have quicker natural senses than others. A coastguardsman, used to surveying the ocean, will detect a tiny boat which would escape the notice of the average landsman; the experienced eye of a detective will build up much useful information from the examination of a footprint, or even a handful of ash, which would mean nothing to the ordinary traveler. Similar differences hold in the realm of the soul; many poison their systems without being aware of it.

It is therefore of the utmost importance to exercise the soul in the discriminations of the inner sense, and to accustom it to act on its findings. This was probably in the mind of our Lord when He spoke so earnestly about the rule of the eye, too accustomed to move carelessly over faces and forms, on the spectacle of human and natural life, as it passes in ceaseless panorama before us. It would not have been easy to speak to all the world about the senses of the soul. People would not for the most part have understood Him. But if He could only teach them that there might be sin in a look, and that an unregulated look might lead to sin, it would be at least one step toward awakening the soul to watchfulness against those first yieldings to temptation, which reveal themselves not only in the glance of the eye, but in the inner movement of the soul. Let a man begin to guard his looks, he will end by keeping his heart beyond all else that he keeps, since he has come to see that out of it are the issues of life (Prov. 4:23).

Passionate Desires

We must learn, most of all, to conquer passionate desire. The appetites which God has implanted within us, for food, for sleep, for human love, and such things, are not in themselves wrong, but they are most likely to get wrong in two directions. Either we may desire a right thing too passionately and for the mere pleasure it affords, rather than for the service it will enable us to do to others; or we may desire satisfaction from an object which, for good reasons, is placed outside the circumference of our life.

The presence of such an object may excite the passionate desire of our nature; and, if it should, our Lord says we must not look on it. In this case, the old proverb, "Out of sight out of mind," is our only safeguard. What the eye does not see, the heart will be less likely to desire.

The Master goes further, and says that if we are brought into almost constant contact with an object that tempts us, and if we cannot conquer its inevitable fascination upon our temperament, it would be better for us to pluck it out and cast it away, though it were as precious as an eye and useful as a foot. Of course, the best policy would be to acquire such an elevation and strength of soul that we would be superior to the temptation of any wrong or hurtful snare. When a child is well fed it will not fight with dogs for the garbage of the streets. When we come from standing on the Transfiguration Mount, with the light of its recent glory on our faces, we shall find no attractions in the vanities of Vanity Fair. But, failing that, and as the next best thing, it is wiser, like Joseph of old, to leave our garment and flee, refusing even to be in the same room with the temptress (Gen. 39). At whatever cost, however, we must learn to master the desire of our senses, and not allow our feet to wander in the direction they solicit, unless it be one which God Himself has marked out for us. Even then we must tread in it with moderation, such as is imposed on the one side by the remembrance that every good and perfect gift is the Father's gift, and therefore to be used reverently; and, on the other, by the fear lest we should injure another, and forget that in every act we must consider the well-being of all around us as paramount to our own enjoyment.

It must be, of course, always borne in mind that sin is not to be imputed to the body. It is not the eye that sins, but the heart that uses it for its sin. It is not the body that yields itself to the entrance of evil things, but the soul that turns the key, unlocks the door, and permits sin to enter. No doubt the body is a weight in the heavenly race, because in its subtle nervous mechanism it carries the record and impulse of many acts of unrestrained evil by our ancestors. It is a chain whose links have been forged by many separate acts, which have grown into habits. But the ultimate power is always invested in one's spirit, which must always utter its *I will!* or its *I will not!* before an act can be done which has any moral quality in it, of which we must give an account, and which is either a step toward heaven or toward the pit.

If you sin, it is not your body that sins, but *you* through your body; and you are transforming into a pigsty what God made for His palace and temple. Strong as heredity may be, you are stronger. Vehement as the steeds are which are yoked to the chariot of life, the beneficent Creator would never have given them to you except that He knew that you were well able, with His grace helping you, to rein them in, and compel them to keep the course, run the race, and win the goal. If then you want to arrest acts of sin in your body, it is imperative that you should deal with the inward sense and with the desires of your mind.

Purifying One's Desires
How then can we purify the desires of the mind?

(1) We must *guard against the first tiny thought of evil.* The microbes float in the air, and if at any time we are off our guard and allow them to alight, they will infallibly find a nest in which to breed. The Holy Spirit, if we entrust Him with the sacred task, will make us very sensitive when the tiniest speck of evil is floating toward us, and will remind

us to seek shelter under the Blood. You may shrink from my using that mystic word, but, believe me, there is no other infallible talisman of victory. "They overcame . . . by *the Blood* of the Lamb" (Rev. 12:11).

(2) We must *avoid the occasions of temptations.* It is useless to ask God not to lead us into temptation if we thrust ourselves thither. I had once to advise a young artist to give up painting figures because it was impossible for him to go through the training, which is held to be necessary, without being overmastered by temptations incident to that line of study. It was the right foot, but it always made him stumble, and it had to go. At another time I had no alternative but to advise a young girl to break away from an attachment dear to her as life, because she could not continue it without serious spiritual danger. It was the right eye, but it had to be plucked out. But are these losses without compensation? Nay, verily. It is impossible to give up such things for Christ without receiving a hundredfold in this present life. When Milton's eyes were closed on the scenes of earth they were opened on the Throne of God and the Lamb. We are completed in Him. We go maimed *into Life!*

(3) We must *appropriate the opposite grace.* It is good, but it is not enough to turn the eyes away from beholding vanity, nor to shut them as the ascetic might do from all that is right and natural and innocent. There is something better, supplied by the universal principle, which we are using throughout these chapters—Love.

When our hearts are filled with love, our eyes will not gaze on an object for selfish enjoyment. They will look on the interests of another; will see all the agony and pain that may ensue if that other is turned away, as poor Bathsheba was from the path of righteousness; will fill with tears at the very thought of bringing shame and dishonor into another's life; will become tender with a holy and selfless love; will be yielded as organs of Christ's own vision; and, out of all *that*, will come the transparency of a pure heart, which the Holy Spirit shall make His abiding place.

"Who among us can dwell with the devouring fire" of the Divine purity? He that "shutteth his eyes from looking upon evil, he shall dwell on high" (Isa. 33:14-16, ASV).

CHAPTER NINE

SIMPLICITY IN SPEECH

(Matt. 5:33-37)

Speech! What is it? The vibration of the air set in motion by vocal chord, tongue, and lip. Apparently mechanical, yet how spiritual. Enriched from the voices of nature, the dash of the breaker, the murmur of the breeze, the song of the bird, and the cry of the beast, yet in its original fountains the evident gift of the Creator.

Speech is the utterance of the soul, and more; because the soul dyes and impregnates human speech with its emotions and inspirations, so that they are communicated to others as if by spiritual magnetism. Even when the words themselves are unintelligible we may catch some Divine knowledge, or else our steps may be quickened by the clarion appeal of speech.

God spake, and the visible Creation emerged from the realm of thought into realized fact. By speech the Law was promulgated from Sinai; and by speech He who spake as never man spake, and who was the Word of God incarnate, left us thoughts that can never die. Speech has burned with the vehemence of Demosthenes, flashed with the eloquence of Cicero, trembled with the pathos of Chrysostom, thundered with the emphasis of Luther, rung with the high note of Pitt, glittered with the brilliance of Sheridan, and poured like a torrent from the lips of Burke. What a wonderful gift is human speech. To what heights it may rise, to what depths descend. "Therewith bless we the Lord and Father, and therewith curse we men, who are made after the likeness of God. Out of the same . . . fountain" comes both "sweet water and bitter" (James 3:9-11, ASV).

Speech, Pure and Simple

The noblest form of speech is the reflection in simple and natural words of great and good thoughts which have been occupying the speaker's mind. Then language becomes strong in its simplicity and majestic in its unadorned truth. There is small need for nicely balanced sentences or highly flavored speech when the soul of a patriot, orator, or preacher is aglow with exalted and inspiring conceptions. The volcanic fires that are burning within vent themselves in burning syllables, which plow their way into the hearts of people. When a speaker is deeply moved, his manuscript is crumpled in his hand, the precise words which he had carefully prepared are forgotten, and he makes a fresh way for himself in words that leap red-hot and alive from his lips.

The yeas and nays of Christ have been sufficient to revolutionize the ages, not because of their eloquence (as judged by human standards), but because they are weighted with the wisdom and life of God. Terse, unadorned, and simple sentences—such, for instance, as Abraham Lincoln was wont to utter—are sufficient when far-reaching and profound principles of personal conduct or public policy are announced.

If then we would obey this command of our Lord as to speech, and confine ourselves to pure and simple language, we must begin to think more deeply, to love more tenderly, to cultivate our souls to nobler issues, and to amass spiritual treasure. We can safely leave our words to take care of themselves if our inner lives are pure, and sweet, and strong. Let us only imbibe our Master's spirit, and love God first and our neighbors as ourselves—then from the pure fountain will flow pure streams like those that issue from the throne of God and of the Lamb.

Vows and Other Extravagant Speech

It must, however, be sorrowfully confessed that for the most part the thinking of ourselves and of others is not of that order. People are not usually true, or deep, or unselfish, in their innermost hearts, and they know it, and therefore in all ages they have endeavored to atone for the poverty of their thought by the extravagance of their language.

People are not *true*. To compensate, therefore, for their lack of veracity, and to induce others to think that they were neither lying nor deceiving, they have linked their words with the awesome name of God, daring the All-True to step out of His silence to confound them if it were not as they said.

People are not *profound*. To compensate, therefore, for their lack of deep and original thoughts, and to turn public attention from their threadbare and impoverished souls, they employ extravagant and exaggerated speech, like that with which a frivolous girl is accustomed to expressing herself when for the first time she stands in the presence of the solemn majesty of the Alps at flush of dawn or under the touch of the silver moon.

People are not *unselfish*. To compensate, therefore, for their conscious lack of that love which forgets itself in its devotion to the interests of others they will fill their speech with extravagant expressions, which may impress the ear and heart of those that hear them for the first time, but fall vain and insipid on those who know that the love which vaunts itself most passionately is more than likely to be scheming for its personal advantage.

It is common enough for us to hide our nakedness, our untruthfulness, our selfishness, under strong affirmations and protestations, which call in the Supreme Being to witness against us if it be not as we affirm.

The remarkable thing is that God keeps silent. Though His verdict be invoked by the habitual liar and blasphemer who swears that black is white, and calls on God to strike him dead, or in some other way to prove that his words are false, yet Heaven makes no sign. No voice speaks out of the silence; no thunderbolt hurtles through the air; no sign is given that God is being mocked. Indeed it might seem as though God had not heard, or that He was perfectly indifferent.

But such is not the case. There are many examples on record, like that, for instance, of Ananias and Sapphira, where, in answer to some blasphemous appeal, God has interposed to vindicate the truth which had been shamefully misstated. God is not indifferent. He is not careless of the interest of truth and righteousness. But He usually hides Himself under the slow working of immutable laws. However, He is never appealed to without sooner or later answering the appeal, vindicating innocence and exposing the liar and the profane. With slow, silent, and inexorable precision the Divine Government deals with all exaggerations, lies, and blasphemies, showing their hollowness, exposing their futility, and casting them up on the beach of the universe, to the derision of all pure and righteous souls.

In order to avoid using the Name of God in their protestations, people have introduced into their speech expressions which, in fact, derived all their significance from their association with Him. It has been a mean subterfuge. They have not liked to say, *By God*, or *By the Life of God*, and therefore they have substituted the phrase, *By Heaven*. They are too scrupled to say, *May God strike me dead if I lie*, and therefore they have slightly modified their speech, and said, *By my life*, or *By my head*, though they know that life and death are ultimately only at the disposal of God.

In our own speech we inherit some of these subterfuges, and apparently employ them without thought:

Zounds is a contraction of "By the wounds of Christ."

My dear, or *Dear me*, is an English form of the Italian, Dia mia, my goddess.

Good gracious, or *My gracious*, are clearly abbreviations of "My gracious God."

By Jove is, of course, the Latin name for Divinity.

Begad is "By God."

Many similar expressions will occur to the minds of my readers, and they all savor of the attempt to give the impression of solemnity and reliableness to statements which have no other claim for consideration except that they are associated with the awesome Name and Being of God.

A Simple Lifestyle

The Jews, like all Oriental nations, were especially given to these expletives, and sheltered themselves with the excuse that, so long as they did not mention the Divine Being, they might be excused. They said "Thou . . . shalt perform *unto the Lord* thine oaths" (Matt. 5:33) meant that oaths which were not definitely made to the Lord, or by the invocation of the name of God, were not binding.

Our Lord shows the fallacy of this reasoning. He says that, whatever emphasis the allusions to Heaven, or Jerusalem, or the head, may give to our speech, is derived from their association with God; and that, therefore, if we would avoid the charge of blasphemy, we must cease to interlard our speech with such expressions. They are needless when our hearts are pure and our words sincere; they are objectionable, and worse, when introduced to give a false and unnatural emphasis to our speech.

As the disciples of Jesus, we must avoid, in dress, in expenditure, in our household equipment, whatever savors of extravagance. In all our behavior, as well as in our speech, there must be the simplicity and beauty of Jesus Christ.

Perhaps there is more truth than we would care to admit in the following minute of an old Friends' meeting: "It is the judgment of Friends that we should refrain from having fine tea tables set with fine china, seeing it is more for sight than service, and it's advised that Friends should not have so much china or earthenware set on their mantel pieces or on their chests of drawers, but rather set them in their closets until they have occasion to use them. And we desire an alteration in those things that Truth's testimony is gone out against, namely, the Friends' gowns made indecently, one part over long and the other too short, with lead in the sleeves, and that Friends should come to a stability and be satisfied in the shape and compass that Truth leads into without changing as the world changes, also that Friends' clothes may be of a decent modest color, not hair cut or powdered, and neither coives [hairdos] to be made with gathers on the forehead, bordering on the fashion of the world."

Oaths in Court

This prohibition of our Lord, "Swear not at all" (Matt. 5:34), does not, in my judgment, touch on the subject of taking an oath in a court of law or on the assumption of high office. He is simply dealing with the use of expletives in ordinary speech. In His own trial He did not scruple to be put upon His oath. When the High Priest said unto Him, "I adjure Thee by the Living God, that Thou tell us whether Thou be the Christ, the Son of God," Jesus answered, "Thou hast said" (Matt. 26:63-64).

And on one solemn occasion the Apostle Paul deliberately called God to witness that he spoke the truth in Christ, his "conscience . . . bearing . . . witness in the Holy Ghost" (Rom. 9:1).

It is admissible that on occasions of high and solemn importance we should bare our heads as we stand before God and solemnly ask Him to stand with us in attesting the truth of the words we speak and the vows we make. But there is a vast difference between this and the incessant and thoughtless appeal to God on every small and frivolous occasion.

Proper Respect for God

The true and holy soul finds God everywhere and in everything. Heaven above is God's throne; earth beneath, His footstool; Jerusalem, the holy city, the residence of the great King (Matt. 5:34-35). Note these closing words—"the Great King." We are reminded of the sublime words with which the last of the prophets rebuked the lax and slovenly worship of the chosen people: "From the rising of the sun even unto the going down of the same My Name shall be great among the Gentiles; and in every place incense shall be offered unto My Name, and a pure offering. . . . For I am a great King, saith the Lord of hosts, and My Name is dreadful among the heathen" (Mal. 1:11, 14).

Let us cultivate this thought, that God is not only our Father, but a great King, and with all the familiarity of little children will be mingled reverential awe. Wherever we go we shall recollect the presence of God, and this will prevent us from the spirit which is betrayed into extravagant speech. We shall not dream of using words which come within the scope of our Lord's condemnation when we remember that every word is spoken in the presence of our Judge, and that of every idle word that we may speak we shall be called to give an account (Matt. 12:36).

All harsh judgments of other people, who are God's creatures; all flippant reference to Scripture to spice our conversation, including witticisms and conundrums; all light remarks on God's dealings with people, as in a book once published, called "The Comic History of England"; all trifling with sacred subjects, or exposing them to ridicule— will be impossible to those who invest them with the thought that God is great, and greatly to be feared, and to be held in reverence by all that are about Him.

The reverent use of the Day of God; the entrance with devout and sacred thoughts into His House; the wary and careful participation in the Lord's Supper; the loving handling of Scripture, and even of the Book which contains it; the honor with which parent and friend, old and young, are treated—all these admirable and beautiful traits, so necessary to the perfecting of character, are due to the same origin and source. When God is treated as the Great King, one's whole life falls into symmetry and order, and becomes a prolonged *Yea* to truth, a profound *Nay* to falsehood and error, to the glory of Him who is God's Yea and Amen to all the needs of the human soul.

CHAPTER TEN

THE SECOND MILE

(Matt. 5:38-42)

It is the second mile that tests our character. About the first there is no controversy. We must traverse it whether we will or not.

Our Lord refers to the usage of the East in the transmission of the royal messages. They are carried forward by relays of messengers, much in the fashion of the Fiery Cross in the Highlands, as Sir Walter Scott describes it in "The Lady of the Lake." But the messengers were conscripted men, that is, each village or township was bound to forward the message to the next, and the first man that was happened on, however pressing his own business, was obliged to use his horses or mules, or go forward on foot with the royal courier, carrying his baggage.

In the same way emergencies are continually happening to us all. We leave our homes in the morning not expecting any demand for help or any other circumstance to interfere with the regular routine of the day's engagements. Then, all suddenly and unexpectedly, there are the sounds of horses' hoofs. A great demand has burst in on our lives, and we are obliged to go off in a direction which we never contemplated. We have no option. We are compelled to go one mile, and then the question will arise: Now that you have performed what you were bound to perform, and given what anyone else would have given, what are you going to do? The next mile is of prime necessity; it is in your option to go or not to go, and your action will determine whether or not you have entered into the inner heart of Christ, and are His disciple, not "in word" only, but also "in deed and in truth" (1 John 3:18).

What about the *left* cheek? That the right one should have been struck is an incident which has happened to you altogether apart from your choice (Matt. 5:39). It does not reveal your character in one way or the other, but your behavior with respect to the left cheek will show immediately what you are.

What about your *cloak?* (Matt. 5:40) Apparently your creditor can claim your tunic, and there is no merit in giving it up—anyone must do this much. But when that is gone, what will you do about your cloak? This is a test of what you really are.

Should We Obey These Words Literally?

But does our Lord mean that we should do literally as He says? Are we really to go the second mile, and turn the left cheek, and let our cloak go in the wake of our coat? These questions have been asked all along the ages, and answered as we answer them still. Each questioner must be fully persuaded in his own mind; and according to your faith, so it will be done unto you.

Many saintly souls have yielded a literal obedience to these precepts. It is recorded of the eccentric but devoted Billy Bray that in going down into the pit, shortly after his remarkable conversion, an old companion gave him a stinging blow on the cheek. "Take that," he said, "for turning Methodist." In former times such an insult would never have been attempted, for the whole country knew that Billy Bray was an inveterate pugilist. All the answer that he gave, however, was, "The Lord forgive thee, lad, as I do, and bring thee to a better mind; I'll pray for thee." Three or four days later his assailant came to him under the deepest conviction of sin and asked his forgiveness.

The head of the constabulary in a great district in India told me that when he became a Christian he found it necessary to withdraw from the Gymkana (which is the European club and society rendezvous in most Indian cities), and his action in this matter aroused very strong feeling against him among his former associates. One day, as he was driving on the highroad, a well-known society man, driving past him in the other direction, rose up in his dog-cart and cut at him a tremendous blow with his whip, saying as he swore, "Take that, you . . . " My friend, who is a very powerful man and of commanding presence, took it quietly, waited his opportunity of doing this man a kindness, and I believe it was the means of his conversion also.

In connection with a missionary society working among the tribes in the Congo, in which I am deeply interested, one of the missionaries resolved that he would teach a literal obedience to these words of our Lord, lest any evasion of them might lessen their authority over the hearts and lives of His people. His hearers were greatly interested and excited, and were not slow in putting the missionary to the test. On one memorable day they gathered around his house, and began asking for the articles which excited their cupidity, and which he had brought at such cost from home. In an hour or two his house was literally stripped, and his wife and he betook themselves to prayer, for, of course, it is impossible for Europeans to live in that climate without many accessories which are needless for the natives. But, in the evening, under the shadow of the night, one after another stole back bringing the articles which he had taken away, and confessing that it was impossible to retain them in his possession, because of the burden which had come upon his heart.

Many such instances are probably occurring every day, and compel us to believe that there is a range of laws which should govern our dealings with our fellows, and which are only unfolded to those who live not by sight, but by faith in the Son of God. Faith has been called the sixth sense, and lays its hands on a third keyboard of the great organ of existence.

Far be it from us, therefore, to judge any people who feel that it is their duty to obey these words of the Master in all literality.

Are There Any Exceptions?

But even if these words are to be taken literally there must be some reserves. For instance, when our Lord says, *Resist not evil* (Matt. 5:39), it is impossible to apply His words universally. Suppose, for instance, as we pass along a road, we encounter a brutal man grossly maltreating a woman or a little child, or a gang of roughs assaulting a fellow traveler. It cannot be that we are forbidden to resist the wrongdoer to utmost of our power. The whole machinery of the eternal and invisible world is continually being called into requisition to succor us against "foul fiends," as Spencer put it, and surely we may do much in these scenes of human existence. Clearly our Lord only forbids us to strike for purposes of private retaliation and revenge; we are not to be avengers in personal quarrels. We are also to guard against taking the law into our own hands lest our passion should drift us outside the warm zone of the love of God.

It is the *personal* element in the resistance of wrong that our Lord forbids; but He would surely never arrest the soldier, policeman, or even the private citizen, from stopping, so far as possible, deeds of wrong and acts of criminal assault. If thieves break into your home, or wicked men should try to injure your wife or child; or you should come on some poor Jew who is set on by robbers who strip him of his property, and beat him almost to death, you are bound to interfere with a prayer to God that He would succor you.

And after the wrong has been done, as the Lord teaches us by His own behavior, we may reprimand and remonstrate and appeal to the conscience and heart. When one of the officers of the court struck Jesus with his hand, Jesus answered him, "If I have spoken evil, bear witness of the evil; but if well, why smitest thou Me?" (John 18:23) But there we must stop. We must not say in our heart, "I will get even with you, and give you as much as you have given me."

It is equally our duty, it seems to me, to take measures to arrest and punish the wrongdoer. Supposing that a man has wronged you, and that you have good reason to believe that he is systematically wronging others; if you have an opportunity of having him punished, you are absolutely obliged, as it seems to me, to take such action against him as will make it impossible for him to pursue his career of plundering. If your lot should be cast in a mining camp in the Far West, which was dominated by some swaggering ruffian, and he assaulted you, I do not think that you would be contravening the law of Christ if you were to give him so strong a handling that his power for evil would be arrested from that hour. It being clearly understood that you put out of your heart all private revenge, all personal malice, and are living in a land where it is impossible to bring the wrongdoer before judge or jury, you may be compelled to act in a judicial capacity, doing for society what society could not do through its legalized officers and methods. Expostulation, argument, appeals to reason, might be employed first; but if these failed there would be necessity to use the only other argument that might be available.

It is clear, also, that we cannot literally obey the Lord's injunction to give to everyone that asks. Else the world would become full of prosperous beggars, who lived on the hard-earned wages of the thrifty. And this would result in the undoing of society, and of the beggars themselves. Does God give to all who ask Him? Does He not often turn aside from the borrower? He knows what will hurt or help us; knows that to many an entreaty His kindest answer is a rebuff; knows that if He were to give us all we ask we should repent of having asked as soon as we awoke in the light of eternity. So when a drunkard or a drone asks me for money I steadfastly refuse. It is even our duty not to give money indiscriminately, and without full acquaintance with the applicant and his circumstances, for we may be giving him the means of forging more tightly the fetters by which he is bound to his sins. A piece of bread is the most we may bestow upon the beggar until we have some knowledge of his character, his mode of life, and his real intentions. If only Christian people would resist the impulse to give money to cadgers of all kinds, and give it to the more modest poor who suffer without making appeals, much evil and sorrow would be remedied!

What Does God Want Us to Do?

What then does the Lord require of us?

(1) *Do not take the law into your own hands.* In the old Mosaic legislation it was enacted that as a man had done, so it should be done to him. "Eye for eye, tooth for tooth, hand for hand, foot for foot, burning for burning, wound for wound, stripe for stripe" (Ex. 21:24-25). But in the time of our Lord this had been interpreted as conferring on a man the right to retaliation and revenge. The Jews conveniently ignored Leviticus 19:17-18, which expressly forbade the private infliction of punishment.

When we are wronged we must refer the wrong to the great organized society of which we are part. Society will lay its hand on the wrongdoer. The judge who sits on the bench is not an individual, but the embodiment of society, the representative of law and order; and if he condemns a fellow creature to penal servitude for life there should be no kind of malice or vindictive feeling in his breast.

(2) *Turn Retaliation into Redemption.* When struck on the cheek the instant impulse of a natural person is to strike back on the cheek of the smiter. There should be a second blow. But the Master says if there be a second blow, let it fall on your other cheek. Instead of inflicting it, suffer it. Instead of avenging yourself on the wrongdoer, compel yourself to suffer a second blow, in the hope that when you offer your uncomplaining patience to his brutality you may effect his redemption. The first blow was of his malice, the second blow will be of your love, and this may set new looms at work within his heart, weaving the fabric of a new life. Thus the wrongs that men have done to God led Him to present the other cheek to them, when He sent them His only begotten Son, "who, when He was reviled, reviled not again; when He suffered, He threatened not, but committed Himself to Him that judgeth righteously" (1 Peter 2:23). The patient sufferings of our Lord have melted the hearts of people; and, as in His case, so in a lesser extent it will be in ours.

(3) *Be large-hearted.* "Freely ye have received, freely give" (Matt. 10:8). Do not be stingy and niggardly in your behavior toward people. You are obliged to yield the coat, also

give the cloak. You are compelled to go for one mile at least, now, out of sincere desire to serve the purposes of the commonwealth, go another. The law compels you to give your cabman a shilling for two miles; but give him an extra sixpence if you go to the extreme margin of that distance. The law compels you to pay your debts; but if you have incurred them, and they are rightfully due, pay them without haggling. There are certain duties in the home which fall to our lot to be performed: do them with a smile; *that is the second mile*. The husband must give the needed money to his wife for household expenditure; let him do it without grudging; *that is his second mile*. The employee must render certain services to his employer. If he renders these with a grudging spirit, doing only what he is paid to do, not entering into the spirit of his work, or doing it to the utmost of his power, he is like an impressed laborer, carrying the messages against his will; but as soon as he does his duty with alacrity and eagerness, even staying overtime to finish a piece of necessary service, *that is his second mile*.

(4) *The Master insists that we should cultivate an ungrudging, unstinting, and generous spirit.* "God loveth a cheerful giver" (2 Cor. 9:7). Think of God in His incessant giving. Giving His sun and His rain; giving to the Church and the miser, the thankless and heartless, as well as to the loving and prayerful. That is to be our great model. We are to be stars, ever pouring our light on the vault of night; flowers, shedding fragrance, though on the desert air; fountains, though we rise in the lonely places of the world, where only the wild things of nature come to drink. Always giving love and help to this thankless and needy world, because we are so sure that as we give, we shall get; as we break our barley loaves and small fishes, our hands will be filled, and filled again, out of the storehouses of God. Freely ye have received, freely give; and in "what measure ye mete, it shall be measured to you again" (Matt. 7:2).

I want to add my testimony to the literal truth of these words. In my life I have found repeatedly that in proportion as I have given I have gotten, and that people have given into my bosom, according to heaven's own measure, pressed down, heaped up, and running over (Luke 6:38).

For all this we need to have a new Baptism of Love. The love of God must be poured into our hearts by the Holy Spirit, who is given unto us. We must learn to unite ourselves with our Father's redemptive purpose, looking at the wrong done to us, not so much from our standpoint, but from that of the wrongdoer, with an infinite pity for all the poisonous passion which is filling his heart, and an infinite desire to deliver and save him. Our thought for his welfare will thus overmaster all desire for our personal revenge, and we shall heap on his head the hot coals of our love, to melt his heart and save him from himself.

CHAPTER ELEVEN

GOD'S PRIMAL LAW

(Matt. 5:44)

What must be done for life—eternal life—the deepest and best? Everyone desires to know that. We all want to drink of the goblet of life, and to drink it to the last drop, to know everything that can be known in the brief limits of our existence, of true enjoyment. Everyone asks the question, in one form or another, How can I taste the inner meaning of life?

This is the answer—Love is life; and everyone who loves perfectly God and his fellows is already drinking of the River of Water of Life that flows from the throne of God and the Lamb.

You may be startled for a moment, having often heard from the lips of teachers and preachers the formula, Believe and Live. Is there then a contradiction when the Master says, Love and Live? No, as you will discover as soon as you endeavor to live a life of perfect love without believing in Christ. You cannot do it. If you could, the Gospel would be needless; but because it is impossible for people to love like this, the Lord Jesus came to renew our natures and teach us to love; yea, He ascended on high to send the Holy Spirit, that He might shed abroad the love of God in our hearts. Love is not indigenous to the children of Adam's race; it must be implanted as an exotic seedling from heavenly soil.

But when we speak of love, we do not mean that it is primarily an emotion of the soul; it is the expression of the soul in action. Love consists in being willing to do. "Thou shalt love the Lord thy God *with all thy . . . strength*" (Mark 12:30). Many are disappointed because they try to love God with their hearts before they make Him first in their wills. Many who begin to serve Him in this way will end in loving Him with warmth and tenderness of sympathy.

It's Not Enough to Love Those Who Love Us

How beautiful it is to see the amenities of human life—one person's trust of another, the love of parent to child, the devotion of wife to husband. These things, like the flowers that festoon unsightly ruins, adorn the lives and characters and homes of some people who lay no claim to godliness. The abandoned woman presses her babe to her breast with maternal pity; the bandit is attached to his comrade, who shares his rug and spoils and plunder; and even the grim tyrant is attached to the woman he calls wife. These virtues are the wild flowers that grow over the rugged natures of people. But they are not the test of our Christian life. If you simply love those who love you, and are kind to those that are generous, and greet those who greet you, you are not doing more than those who act at the prompting of their own human hearts.

The children of God must do more than this. If the religion of Jesus Christ does not lift its professors out of the ordinary level of mankind into an altogether new atmosphere, to stand amid a fresh environment, and to give proof that they have found something which others do not possess—it can boast nothing better than what was yielded by the hoary religions of the past, and is doomed to pass away. No; the Lord demands that, as there are men and women in our social circles whom we naturally dislike, whose temperaments offend us, and whose prosperity is a matter for which we naturally cannot pray, so we cannot attain to His ideal until we have learned to love, pray for, and bless them with a Divine and heaven-born unselfishness.

How many Christians form a false estimate of themselves! Their friends flatter them that are generous and kind, and with such estimates they are only too ready to concur. We judge ourselves by the way in which we behave to wife, child, or friend, to those in our own circles of life, where it is easy to be open in heart and hand. That, however, is far from being an adequate test of what we really are. People of the world can be attractive and winsome under similar surroundings. The only adequate gauge of the quality of our Christian life is furnished by our attitude toward those from whom we are separated by prejudice, temper, or the consciousness of unfair and unkind behavior. These relationships furnish the real test of what we are before God, since we are toward God what we are to them. Such an attitude of kindness and prayerful sympathy is impossible to people of the world. Thus Christ's command is a profound and searching test when He reiterates the ancient Law: *"Thou shalt love thy neighbor"* (Lev. 19:18).

(1) *Every man loves himself.* This is universally true. The whole tendency and drift of human life which has not been regenerated by the Holy Spirit is to revolve around the pivot and center of one's own individuality. This is the result of being born of the first Adam, proving the necessity of being born again of the Holy Spirit.

(2) *Everybody has a neighbor.* This is also taken for granted. You are not only the center of your own life, but part of the circumference of someone else's life. That circumference may be a very wide and far-extended one, but you cannot evade the fact that you have been born into a community or family of people; and, as we shall see, the point is not, who is your neighbor, so much as whom you will neighbor. Any person you shall encounter within the next hour on the king's highway who needs your help is your neighbor.

(3) *The world's method is at variance with God's.* The children of this world try to limit as far as possible the number of their neighbors, and to admit as few as possible within the pale of their generosity; whereas God's principle is to go forth to all who need comfort and help. A lawyer asked, "Who is my neighbor?" (Luke 10:29), hoping that Christ would limit the duty of neighborliness within as narrow

limits as possible—a blood relation, or such like. But our Lord always taught that we were to be on the lookout to prove our neighborliness. Go through the world proving as far as possible your neighborliness. The lawyer asked, "Who is my neighbor?" But the Lord answered, "Go, and show yourself a neighbor."

Remember Three Characteristics of Everyone

(1) *Every man has his rights.* There are his *inherited* rights, such as his right to freedom; for no one should enslave his fellow, and everyone in whose heart there is a part of God's love is bound, so far as he may, to secure liberty for the enslaved. Everyone has a right also to fresh air, fresh water, sufficient land for the maintenance of life (whether cultivated by himself or by others is not material). Everyone also has a right to freedom of conscience; so that nobody is justified in imposing his creed or manner of Divine worship on another.

These are rights which every individual member of the human family has a claim to; and, if we would live a life of perfect love, we must respect these rights in every man, though a beggar; in every woman, though a servant.

We all have *acquired* rights, such as those of character and of reputation. No one has a right to take another's character or impair his reputation. If there is some blemish in another's character which calls for reprehension and blame, dare to tell it him between himself and yourself; but do not filch away his reputation.

There are also the rights of *property.* These must be respected. Anything like a *compulsory* division of property is impossible to Christ's disciples, though we all may proceed on the *voluntary* principle which was practiced by the early Church, and of which the early chapters of the Acts tell so wonderful a story. Directly, as we begin to live the life of perfect love, we begin to respect the rights of another, and to care for them as if they were our own.

(2) *Everyone has his necessities.* How infinite the variety of need! The employer needs the employee quite as much as the employee the employer. We are bound to each other by a network of necessities, and a person in whose heart is

God's perfect love learns to minister to those needs, whatever they may be and whenever there is an opportunity—it being always remembered, of course, that one may be compelled to turn aside from some needs he would like to meet because of the call of other and more urgent ones.

A recent writer has contrasted the demand of Christ with the demand of the world, as the contrast between ministry and mastery. The devil says, "Ye shall be as gods" (Gen. 3:5). Christ says, "Be ye therefore perfect, as your Father . . . is perfect" (Matt. 5:48). But, in order to be as gods, the devil says you must be prepared to trample people beneath your feet. Christ says, "If thou wilt be perfect, go and sell that thou hast, and give to the poor, and thou shalt have treasure in heaven" (Matt. 19:21). The difference is that one set of people go blustering over the world showing their strength, and insisting on other people serving them; while the other set are perpetually giving themselves away in ministry, losing their souls to find them.

(3) *Everyone has his sins.* We often seem to forget how clearly Christ has laid down our duty about our behavior to others. "If thy brother . . . trespass against thee" (Matt. 18:15), what do you do? You are cool to him, do not speak to him, give him a wide berth. He has done you a wrong, and you tell your wife and children to have no friendly contacts with his wife and children. If you meet him in the street, you may nod stiffly and pass. But Jesus says, "Go and tell him his fault between thee and him alone" (Matt. 18:15).

Go? Let *him* come to *me.* Go? Why should I? If he should be in need or at the point of death I would go, but why should I go now?

Yet the Lord would have you go, and go now, that you may gain and win your brother to a better mind. Ah, you will never do it until you have learned to love.

Yet another text says, "If a man be overtaken in a fault, ye which are spiritual, restore such an one" (Gal. 6:1). Too often we whisper to this and the other the story of his sin, saying, "Of course you will not tell." But that is not God's way. No, says the Lord; lovingly lift that fallen man or woman up again in the spirit of meekness, remembering how easily tempted you are, too. Then go to your place of secret prayer, and pray God that you may not be tempted to your undoing, and, if you are, that someone's love should do for you what your love has done for him.

Once more, "If any man see his brother sin a sin which is not unto death, he shall . . . pray" (1 John 5:16). Instead of talking of it, let us hasten away to a secret place and cry to God. What will be the result? God "shall give him life for them that sin not unto death." And the one who has sinned shall feel life coming back into his soul. He may not know why, but in heaven he will discover that it was because his brother, who saw the act, went away and prayed for him. Why do we not act thus? Ah! We need "the love of God . . . shed abroad in our hearts by the Holy Ghost which is given unto us" (Rom. 5:5).

CHAPTER TWELVE

"PERFECT AS GOD"

(Matt. 5:43-48)

Ⅰn the garden the serpent suggested to our first parents that they should be as God, in knowing good and evil; but the Master tells us that we are to be as God in the character and temper of our inner lives. If His words here are compared with the parallel ones in Luke 6, we discover that He desires us to resemble our Heavenly Father, not in our knowledge—which would, of course, be impossible—but in our love and mercy. The perfection on which He insists is a perfection of love. Our natures are, of course, limited in extent and shallow in depth as compared with the ocean fullness of the Infinite God; but a cup may be in its measure as brimming full as an ocean when the tide is high. Up to our measure we may become as full of Love as, in His far greater measure, our Father is; and this is what Christ demands when He says: "Be ye therefore perfect, even as your Father which is in heaven is perfect" (Matt. 5:48).

The Law, Love, and Hate

This is the fifth illustration which He gives, that He is come, not to destroy, but to fulfill the Law by shedding abroad in our hearts that love which is the fulfilling of that Law; and it is interesting to notice exactly the change which

He wrought in the ancient code.

The precept which our Lord quotes: "Thou shalt love thy neighbor and hate thine enemy," cannot be found in the Old Testament. On the contrary, its pages are strewn with the most moving exhortations to love. If any of my readers would take the pains to investigate the matter, they would be startled to find the numerous exhortations to love which are scattered through the ancient code—generally considered so rigorous and severe. "If," said Moses, "thou meet thine enemy's ox or his ass going astray, thou shalt surely bring it back to him again." And again: "If thou see the ass of him that hateth thee lying under his burden, and wouldest forbear to help him, thou shalt surely help with him" (Ex. 23:4-5). In a later age the same kindly spirit appears in the injunction of the preacher: "Rejoice not when thine enemy falleth, and let not thine heart be glad when he stumbleth, lest the Lord see it, and it displease Him" (Prov. 24:17-18). When, therefore, our Lord said: "Ye have heard that it hath been said, 'Thou shalt love thy neighbor and hate thine enemy,' " He did not mean to refer to the inspired teachers of His people, but to those later Rabbis and Scribes who had overlaid the pure gold of Moses with their own incrustations.

There were two ways in which the teachers of the corrupt periods of Hebrew history had vitiated the scope of these ancient laws. First, they had obliterated the words "as thyself," and whittled down the precept from "Thou shalt love thy neighbor *as thyself*" (Lev. 19:18), to "Thou shalt love thy neighbor." Next, they had, out of their own bad hearts, added the words, *"and hate thine enemy"*—lowering the Word of God to suit their own tradition.

Was it not high time that the moss and grit of centuries should be removed from the ancient characters which the Spirit of God had cut in the legislation of Sinai, and that Christ should re-edit the old Law, doing away with the hateful additions, and enlarging the significance of that word "neighbor"? They had delighted in limiting it. He rejoiced to level the walls of religious bigotry, jealousy, and national exclusivism, and taught that our neighbor is simply anyone to whom we can show kindness, so that the word stands for the universal brotherhood of man.

Our Lord desires that we should show love and kindness not only to people as people, but equally to our enemies as to our friends; to those who curse, hate, and despitefully use us, as well as to those who will sacrifice everything on our behalf.

Three Needed Inspirations

To enable us to realize such a command He suggests the Inspiration of a great Nature, a great Example, and a great Hope.

(1) *We need the inspiration of a great nature.* "Children of your Father which is in Heaven" (Matt. 5:45); "Children of the Highest" (Luke 6:35). Some people count much on ancestry. To be connected, however distantly, with the greats of bygone times, is a subject of never-ceasing congratulation. To be able to point to some tomb, where the cross-legged effigy on the stone denotes the Knight Templar, or a stone indicates a pilgrim who crossed the seas in the Crusades, is of prouder boast than wealth and lands. To wear a coat of arms, which proves royal affinity—ah, how much is this! And there is ground for it, because descent and blood undoubtedly count for something. When the special call comes there is something in heredity that answers it.

How much then must it count, when we stand face to face with urgent duty, that the capacity for its due discharge is certainly within us by virtue of our relationship to God through Jesus Christ?

We have been born again by the Word and the Spirit. From the family of the first Adam we have become grafted into the family of the second. We who trust in the Son of God are the children of God by faith in Him, and if children then heirs, heirs of God, and joint heirs with Christ (Rom. 8:17). And because we are sons God has sent forth the Spirit of His Son into our hearts (Rom. 8:9). Since, then, we are partakers of the Divine Nature, we have within us the capacity for Divine Love. We may not be aware of its presence within us, but it is there, and if only we would dare to give it exercise, and allow it to make for itself an outlet in our kindly advances toward those who have served us ill, we should find that through the channels of outward expression the very fountains of Divine Love which are within us would pour their crystal tides.

You can love as God, not in quantity, but in quality, because God's own nature has been begotten in you, and awaits the opportunity of approving itself before both people and angels.

(2) *But we need, also, the inspiration of a great example.* Who is there that has not sometimes stood on the mountain of Transfiguration with Moses and Elias? A visit from some celestial nature, a biography, a noble act, a reunion which has revealed depths and emotion that surpass all previous experiences—these have greatly influenced our lives, and made us resolve that life should henceforth be new. And so our Lord brings us face to face with a marvelous illustration of the love which He desires us to show.

Of course, He Himself, as He sat there, was the supreme Instance of God's impartial love. But the time had not arrived when He could speak plainly of Himself; so He selected His example from the humbler book of Nature, which He had often studied in His highland home, and which lies open before nearly everyone's eyes.

It was the month of April. Before His eyes was spread a charming landscape, on which the natural incidents to which He referred were probably taking place at that moment.

As Jesus spoke the sun was shining. It was the Father's sun—"He maketh *His* sun to rise" (Matt. 5:45). It was *His* thought, *His* Creation, the instrument of *His* benediction. "See," said the Master, "how the sun is shining on the children as they play their merry games, and at the same moment on the prison filled with hardened criminals, on the casement of the cottage to revive the sick girl's drooping life, and on the path of the poor fallen one, as she avoids it, and steals into the shade; upon the little patch of ground belonging to the poor widow, which barely affords her a living, and on the acres of the avaricious tyrant, who cares neither for God nor man, and would despoil her of her holding if he could. The sun shines equally on them all."

Then the Master may have pointed toward a heavy rain

cloud, from the Mediterranean, which came trailing over the country, dropping its beneficent showers from its impartial buckets. Yonder lie two fields with but a narrow fence between. That to the right belongs to an atheist of the worst type, who blasphemes God's name, underpays his servants, robs widows, and browbeats the poor. That to the left is the holding of one who is as careful of his religious observances as the other is careless. The swift shadow of the cloud draws near. If it were steered by a human hand, it would probably be guided, so as to leave the one untouched while it poured its stores on the other. But there is no shade of difference in the distribution. The abundant and refreshing showers fall on both sides of the fence.

Life is like an April day. It is not all sun, nor all cloud. The saddest lives have some patches of blue, some hours of sun. The happiest have some showers, and are overspread now and again with shadow. And surely this is best, for those people are not the noblest who always stay on the tableland, and never descend unto the valley of shadow. For *Sun*, you may have had love at home, a happy childhood, a loving wife, sweet children, prosperous years in business, long spells of good health, happy episodes, weeks and months of country or sea. For *Rain*, you may have had seasons of ill health, of business anxiety, and of bereavement. Now, if we were to compare experiences between the men and women of our acquaintance in the same position of life, putting away all considerations of the inner peace of heart which Christianity gives, I do not suppose that in their outward lives there would be much apparent difference. There are thousands of homes where God's name is not honored—where but goodness and mercy, like guardian angels, follow the inmates all the days of their lives. Why? Because the course of events in this world moves by a blind machinery? No. Because God has no special care whether a person is good or bad? No. But because God loves His enemies, blesses those that curse Him, and is kind to the unthankful and unloving. If anything, He seems more bountiful to those who oppose Him most, that by His mercy He may lead them to repentance.

A man will sometimes speak thus: "I am one of the luckiest fellows living; all my dreams have been realized; I have a good wife, have not had an hour's illness, and have never wanted for money." Such people do not realize that it is God who has given them all things richly to enjoy, making no distinction between them and His dearest children, because He is not breaking in upon their shameful neglect of His claims. He gives "rain from heaven and fruitful seasons, filling our hearts with food and gladness," that we may turn from vanity "unto the living God, which made heaven and earth, and the sea, and all things that are therein" (Acts 14:17, 15).

We might, from the experience of such people, edit a new edition of the Parable of the Prodigal in this wise: that when the father in the distant home heard that his son had spent all that he had, instead of letting him come down to the herding of pigs and the eating of their husks, he sent him day by day supplies of sumptuous food, on each hamper of which these words were inscribed, "I love thee still; come home, haste to come home."

But God has given us another and better *Sun* than that which He has hung in heaven's porch. "He commendeth His Love toward us, in that while we were yet sinners, Christ died for us" (Rom. 5:8). And the benefits of the death of the Redeemer are for the world. Therefore it was possible to carry the Gospel, in the first instance, to Jerusalem. The men who had used Him most despitefully lived there, therefore the Master bade His disciples to begin at Jerusalem. "Tell Caiaphas, who sneered at My royalty, that I love him. Tell the gray-haired Annas, the irresolute Pilate, and the mocking Herod, that I desire to bless them. Go and find out the men who drove the nails into My hands and laughed at My dying anguish, and tell them I will pray for them." So the Master left us an example, that we should follow in His steps (1 Peter 2:21).

And God has given another and better *Rain* than that which fertilizes the fields—the rain of the Holy Spirit's influence and grace, which is for the most stubborn and obdurate offenders. Did He not descend in copious effusion upon the city of Jerusalem at the first, though it had but lately crucified the Son, the world's Redeemer? Take heart, you who think that you have grieved Him away, who have done Him despite, who fear that you have committed the unpardonable sin; even to you He comes with a shower of grace, falling with refreshing bounty.

This is the example that we are to follow. Nothing less than God's evenhanded love is to be our model. We are told to be perfect, even as our Heavenly Father is perfect (Matt. 5:48). We are called to be imitators of God, "as dear children," walking "in love, as Christ also hath loved us," even to the point of giving Himself for us (Eph. 5:1-2). Anything short of this is not Christianity as our Lord taught it.

Dr. Abbott has said that he remembers, when he was a boy, sitting by the fireside of a little country inn in Maine, and hearing some men discuss the Sermon on the Mount. They were rough fellows, and one of them, scoffing at Christianity, said, "Thou shalt love thy neighbor—nonsense! It is not in human nature." Exactly; such love is not in human nature. People love those who love them, and greet their friends, and stop there. But it was in Christ's nature, and it is in the Divine nature; and it is in the Divine nature
to be imparted through Christ to those who claim it.

(3) *We require, lastly, the inspiration of a great hope.* What motivates a woman to spend her life on some brutal husband or ungrateful son? Is it not the hope that, at last, her love will conquer? And is it not this, in an infinitely higher sphere, that leads God, our Father, to pour out the ceaseless tides of His heart on the disobedient and rebellious? Does He not see the consummation when the heavens and the earth shall have become new as the result of His unstinted love? And ought not the same purpose to animate us?

It is recorded of a certain Chinese emperor that, on being apprised that his enemies had raised an insurrection in a distant province, said to his officers: "Come, follow me, and we shall quickly destroy them." On his arrival the rebels surrendered to him, and all expected that he would take revenge on them. Instead of this the captives were treated with the utmost humanity. "What!" cried his first

Minister of State, "Is this the manner in which your promise is fulfilled? Your royal word was given that your enemies should be destroyed, and, lo, you have pardoned them all, and even some of them have been caressed."

"I promised," said the Emperor, generously, "to destroy my enemies. I have fulfilled my word, for, see, they are enemies no longer; I have made friends of them."

A Loving Nature

We must henceforth amend our ways, lest we be counted not worthy of Christ. We must rise to the level of His high demands, not in our own strength but His. And let us remember two things: *First*, not to wait for an emotion, but to obey by the sheer power of our will; and, *secondly*, to begin with individuals.

Have we an enemy who is always trying to curse us? We must be willing to bless him with the benediction of our goodwill.

Is there someone in our life who envies and hates us? We must be willing to be kind and good and try to make sure that our behavior is not misinterpreted or hurtful to his independence and moral life.

Is there one who despitefully uses and persecutes us? We must compel ourselves to pray for him, until presently a warm feeling of compassion fills our hearts.

Are there within our reach churlish and bearish people? Let us greet them, when we meet, with Christian courtesy and grace.

Thus you will reach a semblance of *perfection*. It will not be the absolute and infinite perfection of God, for at best it can be only relative and finite. It will not be the perfection of angels, for they have never left their first estate. It will not be a perfection of knowledge, for we are all liable to error. It will not be freedom from temptation, or from such infirmities as weakness of body, dullness of understanding, and incoherence of thought. But it will be after your measure a full-orbed, steady, and loving nature, which shall go through the world shedding sunshine and rain on weary and hopeless souls until they be led to take up heart and hope again.

A little girl gets into a railway carriage. In perfect simplicity she begins to play with some austere-looking man until he relaxes and the two become friends; and from them a genial warmth spreads through the carriage, until everyone begins to talk kindly with his neighbor, and the tedium of the journey is relaxed. Oh, to go through the world like that, with God's radiance on our faces and His love in our hearts! Every day be sunshine or rain to someone, and especially to your enemies, and other people from whom you are naturally repelled.

You say that all this is impossible for you. It is high: you cannot attain unto it. But remember those sweet old words: "When Israel was a child, then I loved him, and called my son out of Egypt . . . *I taught Ephraim also to go*" (Hosea 11:1, 3). Ask your Heavenly Father to teach you to go; to put His Spirit within you as the fountain of His life and love; to work in you to will and to do of His good pleasure.

Everything lies in the will. Are you willing that His will should be done in and through you in respect to the life of love of which we have been treating? If so, then yield yourself to Him, saying, "I cannot be perfect in love, unless Thou dost undertake to realize in me and through me the image of Thine own perfection."

CHAPTER THIRTEEN

THE INWARDNESS
OF TRUE RELIGION

(Matt. 6:1-18)

In the former section of
this wonderful sermon (Matt. 5:17-48) our Lord began by
laying down a general principle (v. 17), and then proceeded
to illustrate it by five particular instances. First, He announced that His attitude toward the Mosaic institutions
was not one of destruction, but of fulfillment; and then He
showed that the love which He had brought to earth would
realize all that Moses asked and more.

The structure of the present section is precisely similar, as
appears from a study of the ASV, which substitutes for
"*Alms*" (Matt. 6:1, KJV) the word "Righteousness," so that
the first verse is a general heading for all that follows. First,
we have the general proposition that righteousness should
not be done for the sake of display; then we have that
principle applied to alms, prayer, and fasting—the three
departments into which the Jews divided their religious life.

The words "Take heed" are searching. We are all tempted to put better goods in the window than we have any-
where else in the shop, and to show better samples than we
can supply in bulk. Three times in these paragraphs the
Lord speaks of "the hypocrites" (vv. 2, 5, 16); and the hypocrite, as the Greek word intimates, is a stage actor. We are
all tempted to perform our religious duties to show them

off before others, and to appear in public arrayed in garments that we do not wear day by day. Our Lord called this spirit "the leaven of the Pharisees" (Matt. 16:6), referring no doubt to the slight and subtle beginnings of this spirit, and its rapid growth, filling one's heart with fermentation and decay. Once you begin thinking you must keep up appearances as a religious person, and try to do so; once you listen, as Simon Stylites, to the murmur of applause which greets you as above the average; once you assume the robes of purity and piety to attract the gaze of your fellows—you have admitted a principle into your heart which not only will rob you of your reward in heaven, but will ultimately eat out all the purity and loveliness from your religious life.

A Show-Off Religion

We Are All Tempted to Outwardness in Religion. Some, of course, seek to acquire a reputation for piety to serve as a cloak for their nefarious purposes. They assiduously weave a rich vestment of alms, prayers, and self-privations, to hide their unhallowed and self-indulgent lives. Such people are, of course, mortified when their religious acts do not come to the front and secure notice. And when they have built up for themselves a great reputation by their charitable deeds, they devour widows' houses and take a mean advantage of their wards. Judas was one of these people; he had built up so great a reputation that none of the other disciples guessed he was about to do the deed of treachery. Beneath the cover of his religious reputation he was able to filch the contents of the bag (John 12:6).

There are others again who, with sincere and transparent motives, began to love and serve God for Himself; but as the days pass they discover that they are regarded as saints, and the sense of being held in reverence by their fellows fascinates them. They become as proud of their grace as other people of their lace, their place, or their race. They realize that they must maintain their reputation at all costs. Of course, the best way to maintain and increase such a reputation is to cease to think about it, and live only for the Lord Jesus; but directly we fail to do this and occupy ourselves with our reputation and the long shadow it casts on the lawn. Then we are tempted to do things, not because God asks them of us, but to resuscitate our waning credit. Our native character is getting a little threadbare, and instead of cleaving closer to God, we put a patch on the elbow or knee by a generous gift, or a call to prayer, or the assumption in tone and manner of special sanctity.

As to Alms (Matt. 6:1-4). The Jews were trained from their earliest days to be merciful and charitable. The law of Moses continually inculcated remembrance of the stranger, the fatherless, and the widow. Liberality to the poor was reckoned as part of religious duty toward God. The prophets never forgot to urge the people to deal bread to the hungry, to bring the outcast home, and to cover the naked. A row of alms boxes stood in the Temple courts to receive the offerings of worshipers; and at every Sabbath morning service appointed officers in the synagogues collected money for the poor of the town, which was distributed the same afternoon. But in our Lord's time many people gave their money to secure merit with God and admiration from others. They bestowed their charity at the doors of the synagogues, where beggars congregated and passers-by could see; or distributed it as they walked along the streets.

Mrs. Judson, in her account of the first Burman convert, says: "A few days ago I was reading with him the Sermon on the Mount. He was deeply impressed and unusually solemn. 'These words,' said he, 'take hold of my very heart. They make me tremble. Here God commands us to do everything in secret, and not to be seen of men. How unlike our religion this is! When Burmans make offerings at the pagodas, they make a great noise with trumpets and musical instruments that others may see how good they are. But this religion makes *the mind* fear God.'"

Probably what has been said of the Jews and Burmans is true of us all. It is apt to make a big difference to our gift if an open plate is handed us, and our money lies open to others' eyes, than if the offering is taken in a bag.

As to Prayer (Matt. 6:5-15). Our Lord, of course, is referring not to social, but private prayer. For most of the day the doors of the synagogues stood open, as the doors of mosques and Roman Catholic churches do; and the Pharisees, at the three hours of prayer observed by all pious Jews, were not content with kneeling in the privacy of their own homes, but deliberately left their homes with the avowed intention and purpose of being seen in the place of public prayer. They took care, also, to be frequently overtaken in the streets, at the hour of prayer, that they might go through their long liturgies of prayer within view of all the passers-by.

Among ourselves the tendency is certainly to conceal, rather than parade, our private prayers; and yet there is a subtle temptation to be more reverent in our demeanor, more careful in saying our prayers and reading our Bibles, when we are in the company of Christian people, than when we are alone.

As to Fasting (Matt. 6:16-18). In the Jewish year were several fast days in addition to the Great Day of Atonement, when the people were to afflict their souls by public fasting. Yet this exercise did not always involve entire abstinence, but often only sacrificing a single meal. But the Pharisees displayed their exceptional piety by exceptional austerities, and carefully let it be known that they were fasting, by gloomy countenances and squalid dress.

Our temptation is certainly not to fast too much, but of never checking our indulgence of appetite in any degree or on any occasion. We would be much healthier and stronger if we sometimes reduced our meals and rested our organs of nutrition. But our temptation comes in another way. We affect a depression, a melancholy, a concern for our country, the state of our churches, the unorthodoxy of certain ministers, or a self-depreciation as miserable sinners, which we do not really feel. It gives us a certain image among our fellows, but it is hypocrisy in the sight of God.

There are some among us who never shed real tears of heartbroken grief before God for the state of things which they pretend to deplore, but who pose among us as Jeremiahs. There are others who never take a glimpse of real and pure fellowship with God or of themselves without rushing into print or speech with it; and while they are passing through such experiences they congratulate themselves that now, at length, they have something worth narrating in the experience meeting or the religious press.

This outwardness of religion is most injurious to us all. Plants subjected to sunlight by day and the electric light by night soon fade. What is the cure for it?

A Filial Spirit

The Cure for Outwardness in Religion Is the Cultivation of a Filial Spirit. Our Lord lived the filial life to its perfection, and shows us what it is. Notice how all His thoughts seem to run up into the one absorbing central thought of the "Father, which art in Heaven" (Matt. 6:9). He is *your* Father—*His* relationship to each soul is personal. He is in secret, and is "thy Father, which seeth in secret," and He waits "to reward . . . openly" (v. 18).There is no need of vain repetitions with Him, because He knows what we need. All prayer is to be directed to Him. It is He who forgives sins. It is He who clothes and feeds ravens, lilies, and His children. From beginning to end this chapter is full of the Father, who was the One Spectator and Audience before whom our Lord lived His earthly life.

Not only did our Lord paint the blessedness of that filial life, but He came to give it to us all. This is what we are called to know, and He has the power to make it ours. Let us ask Him to do this great thing for us here and now. To them who receive Him He gives the privilege of becoming "sons of God, even to them that believe on His Name" (John 1:12), and because we are sons, God sends "the Spirit of His Son" into our hearts (Gal. 4:6). Then the Father finds the child, and the child finds the Father; such closeness of intimacy ensues from this finding that the Father's smile and good pleasure become all the reward that the child cares for. Oh, let us never be content until, in our inner experience, God our Father becomes All in All!

Then we shall never think of showing off our righteousness before people. We shall be good, not to win the approval of our conscience; not because we are inspired by an abstract love of virtue, as climbers may be ambitious to climb to some hitherto inaccessible peak; not even out of regard for the welfare of others—but because we desire, above all things, to please the Father who is in secret. Our Christianity will thus become a sacred inward secret. We shall boldly enter the Holiest of All by the blood of Jesus, and shall dwell in the secret place of the Most High. Even when no earthly temple invites us, we shall enter the temple of our own heart and find God waiting there, in those hidden depths below consciousness, and there shall worship Him, who is Spirit, in spirit and in truth.

To the Christian, it has been truly said, so far as any influence on his moral condition is concerned, privacy and publicity are words without meaning. He acts before others as he does alone, and acts alone as he does before others; for he is never "alone" from that one Spectator, who sees in secret, and whom he seeks to please. One presence fills, possesses, and dominates him.

An Open Heart toward God

Do you know what this is? Since I have been forbidden to use my eyes for reading in a railway train, I have learned some wonderful lessons along this line. Sitting quietly in the carriage I have sought to unite myself with God, not asking Him to help me, but asking if I may help Him; not seeking His sanction on my schemes, but seeking that I may enter into His Redemptive purposes for those whom I love, for His Church and the poor, hungry, needy world. It has been a fruitful experience, and I see how it is possible so to cultivate the sense of the presence of God, and the endeavor to know what is passing in His heart and thought, that one's absorbing impression tends to be of Him, and His will, and His good pleasure.

We must cultivate this openness of heart toward God. There must be no lie in our life, no lack of transparency or sincerity, no concealment or withholding. All the secrets of heart and life must be naked and bare before the eyes of Him with whom we have to do (Heb. 4:13). We must watch against any attempt to seem more and better than we are. We must guard our life in secret as our most sacred jewel. And before we give, or pray, or fast, there must be the quiet gathering of the soul up before God, the silencing of every voice, the dimming of all footlights, the descent into those deepest depths which no eagle's eye has seen. Thus God will become the supreme Object of our endeavor, as we admonish ourselves, "My soul, wait thou only upon God, for my expectation is from Him" (Ps. 62:5).

The manifestation of this inward fellowship will be instantly and abundantly manifest.

(1) *We Shall Realize the Brotherhood of the Filial Life.* When we are near God we shall begin to be occupied with the condition of His children—our brethren and sisters; we shall look upon all our possessions as given us in trust by Him for them; we shall ask what He would have us expend on His behalf. Almsgiving will at once become a sacred thing, into which the stranger may not intrude—it is entirely a matter between the Father and His child. Even the left hand knows not what the right hand gives.

Christian charity is not alms in the usual acceptation of the term, but the service of the Father. Indeed, Christ belittles the alms, and thinks only of the Father's glory and pleasure. Alas, that the Christian Church has reversed this, magnifying the alms and not stopping to inquire the motive. What has been the result? Millions have been given, but the miseries of the world are no less. We have pauperized and demoralized many whom, with the best intentions, we meant to help. Before our alms can really help people we must get on our Lord's level. The alms must be fed from love to God, as an inland lake is fed from some secret creek, which pours from faraway mountains.

(2) *We Shall Become Identified with the Father's Purposes.* Our hearts are deeply wrought upon as we continue in this blissful fellowship, until they pour themselves out in prayer. "Ye people, pour out your heart before Him" (Ps. 62:8). But we no longer pray for our way or plans. Instead we say: "Thou art holy and precious to me; I want to see Thee revered and loved; I desire that others shall see what I see; I find Thy will my heaven, and long to see all resistance and indifference brought to an end." Then daily bread, forgiveness, and deliverance from temptation, become means to the one common purpose and goal of our choice.

The soul that really gets quiet before God, realizing that

He is in secret, is compelled to pray thus. You might as well stop the tide from flowing, birds from song, and children from laughter, as stop that soul from prayer.

> Prayer is the Christian's vital breath,
> The Christian's native air.

(3) *Radiancy of Joy.* We may in our hearts be laying aside this and the other weight. But we know there is no merit in it. We only desire to lessen the influence of the flesh, to promote the vigilance and clear vision of the spirit. It is entirely a matter between God and us, of which we breathe no word to others; and when we meet others there is a gladness on our faces, and a ringing joy-note in our voices, that greatly commend the Gospel of our Lord.

Is there enough of this anointed head, and the face from which all marks of tears have been removed, in our modern Christian life? How often we make no effort to be happy, and make the best of things. We have had a bad night, and have no scruple about imposing our miseries on all around the breakfast table. We have a great anxiety gnawing at our heart, and we affect the appearance of bearing a heavy burden. I suppose there is in all of us a longing to be the object of our friends' solicitude; and there are times when we may freely unburden ourselves to get advice and sympathy; but we have no right to add unduly to the sorrows and anxieties of others, or to the travail of the world.

The life which is hid with Christ in God is a very radiant one, because it hands over all its burdens and anxieties to the Father in secret, and leaves them with Him. Thus it is at leisure from itself to enter into the anxieties of others.

What the future rewards may be of that inner life I do not care to speculate, and what the present rewards are, words fail to tell. The reward of the hypocrite is the gaping wonder of spectators, who smile, criticize, and forget. The reward of the soul that lives with God in secret consists not in thrones or crowns of gold, but in a growing sense of nearness, of affinity, and of mutual understanding, which issue also in a growing likeness, though the saint knows not that his face shines (Ex. 34:29).

CHAPTER FOURTEEN

THE DISCIPLES' PRAYER

(Matt. 6:9-15)

Devout people, as their lives unfold, increasingly turn to prayer—not *prayers* in the plural, but *prayer* in the singular; therefore Psalm 90, which seems to register the mature experience of Moses, ends with the prayer, "Let Thy work appear unto Thy servants, and Thy glory unto their children. And let the beauty of the Lord our God be upon us" (Ps. 90:16-17). It was as though after a long life of intense activity, in which the Great Lawgiver had borne the people on his bosom as a father, and when the activities of his life were drawing to a close, he was impelled to turn to prayer and catch up the yearnings, desires, and purpose of his life in one constant petition.

As we grow older our prayers tend to become simpler and shorter, and more after the method of the Lord's Prayer, which is so short and yet so deep; so brief that we may say it within three minutes, and yet so comprehensive and concise that to be able to say it from the heart continually is the very consummation and climax of the Christian life.

The Lord's Prayer might be more fitly known as the Disciples' Prayer, but it bears forevermore the Master's touch. It has been said that it was not original, and that these phrases had been on the lips of godly men in a former time. We cannot be surprised at that, because our Lord often meditated upon the prayers of Psalmists and Prophets, appropriating them to His own needs, and weaved them into His own communion with the Father. But if the materials were furnished Him from ancient quarries, this prayer is the structure of His own thought; and as we tread its stately aisles, so severe in their simplicity, so majestic in their strength and far distances, we cannot but think of the myriads who have stood on the same pavement, being molded by the same sentences and thoughts, and have found in these seven short but comprehensive petitions sufficient expression for their deepest, holiest moments. Lonely sufferers and crowded congregations; little children just clasping their hands in prayer and the saintly leaders of the Church; the Roman Catholic and the Protestant; the Anglican and the Nonconformist; the servant and his master—all their differences of creed or station, sex or nationality, are forgotten, as they enter to stand together within the precincts of this exquisite and noble structure. It is resonant with their voices, saturated with their tears, and ringing with their adorations. If, therefore, it may be called the Lord's Prayer because He wove together the golden threads of olden time into the exquisite pattern which for symmetry and beauty cannot be surpassed, it may also be called the Disciples' Prayer because in its use the whole Church has become one.

Twice during our Lord's ministry He recited it. In the first instance it was from the Mountain of Beatitudes in His manifesto to His disciples and the great world of men. On the second occasion He had been praying in a certain place, perhaps at early dawn. While His disciples beheld Him rapt in devotion they probably remained at a reverent distance; but when He ceased they came to Him, and one, as spokesman for the rest, said, "Lord, teach us to pray" (Luke 11:1). What a beautiful illustration of the power of unconscious influence! Christ does not appear to have been constantly insisting on the necessity of prayer, but He was constantly praying Himself. His followers knew that in the early morning He would depart into a solitary place for prayer; and they could recall nights in which He had sent them to their homes, while He climbed the mountain slopes to be alone with God; and had they not seen the results in the transfiguring glory that stole upon His face, the composure with which He passed through scenes of turmoil, defeating the power of demons? What wonder that they desired to possess this sacred talisman of prayer! Happy will it be for the Church and the world when the glories of true devotion will be so apparent that people shall be attracted by the evident gains of it to say, "Teach us also to pray."

These concise and beautiful petitions may therefore be used as a form of Prayer. In Luke the preface is, "When ye pray, say" (Luke 11:2). In Matthew the preface is, "After this manner [or fashion] pray ye" (Matt. 6:9). *It seems undoubted, then, that our Lord meant His disciples to use these very words, "When ye pray, say."* Crises often arise in our experience when we are glad enough to know exactly what to say. It is a good thing to have a mold into which to pour the molten metal of fervent hearts. And sometimes, when the spirit of prayer is burning low, the soul will catch fire at the expressions used by those that have preceded it, and will then sweep up into the presence of God in horses and chariots of fire. Forms of prayer may be used as aids to devotion, but they must never become substitutes for the free outpouring of the soul.

But probably the loftiest use of this prayer is as a model. It tells us the sort of petitions we ought to offer, and their fit and fair proportion to each other. We learn that requests for life's sustenance may fairly have a place in our daily prayer; we are perfectly right in talking freely to God about the recurring demands of food and clothes, about the common round, the daily task; but only one place in seven is to be given to these. Three are to be devoted to the needs of our inner life, and the rest are to be surrendered to adoration and intercession. Then again we learn that our requests for ourselves should always be subordinate to those we make for the coming of the Kingdom and the Hallowing of the Name. These come first in prayer, and they should come always first in our thoughts and lives. This prayer, therefore, seems to be a kind of copybook.* At the head of each page there stands a petition on a copperplate printing for us to go over, repeating it exactly; and below there is a blank sheet for us to fill in with petitions of our own, formed on the model of that at the head of the page, and yet as different as the Spirit of God and the exigencies of the moment may suggest.

Four Suggestions for Prayer

"OUR FATHER WHICH ART IN HEAVEN" (Matt. 6:9). *We may obtain some general suggestions for prayer:*

(1) *Prayer should be direct.* The Jewish proverb said, "Everyone who multiplies prayer is heard." They would babble forth a monotony of unmeaning sound, as the Mohammedans incessantly repeat "Allah," and the Hindus for days together repeat the monosyllable "Om." And it was this senseless, unmeaning repetition of words which our Lord forbade. "Use not vain repetitions as the heathen do" (Matt. 6:7). Let your petitions be simple, direct, intelligent. Say what is in your heart concisely, thoughtfully, earnestly. Come to your Father as a child, and tell Him all your desires, and, having made your definite requests known, await the definite replies which He will certainly send. "Thy Father which seeth in secret shall reward thee openly" (Matt. 6:6).

Of course there are hours in all lives of Gethsemane agony when the soul can only lie low and crushed before God, unable to formulate many petitions, and only able to repeat again and again feebly the name of Jesus, or the phrase He used so often in the hour of His own sorrow, *"Thy will be done."* But this experience makes laws to itself. For the most part we must be careful not to pray by rote or by the clock. A prayer which occupies, as this does, only three minutes to repeat, is prayer.

(2) *Prayer must be reverent.* Reverence is suggested by the words, "which art in heaven." Far be it from me to say a single word to discourage that holy familiarity with which the child of God approaches the Father. The tenderest words, the completest confidence, the closest intimacy, will be welcomed and reciprocated. But let it ever be remembered that the mercy seat is a throne, and the Father a

---

*A book formerly used in teaching penmanship and containing models for imitation.

Great King. His abode is not only a home, but a palace, on whose floors angels tread with reverence, or, standing, veil their faces with their wings. Let us hesitate for a moment on the threshold of our prayers and reverently unloose our shoes from off our feet. Be not rash with thy mouth, and let not thine heart be hasty to utter anything before God; for God is in heaven, and thou upon earth" (Ec. 5:2).

(3) *Prayer must be unselfish.* "When ye pray," do not say I, me, mine, but *we, us, our.* Not my Father, but *our* Father. Instead of teaching in abstract phrases the duty of intercession, the Lord so weaves it into the structure of this prayer that no one can use it without becoming a priest and pleading for others. It is remarkable how, on the one hand, our Lord insists on lonely prayer, "Enter into thy closet and when thou hast shut thy door, pray to thy Father which is in secret" (Matt. 6:6); and yet a moment after He shows that that secret prayer should not be selfish prayer, but linked with the needs of the great family outside the closet door. The prayer that does not recognize the needs of others as well as its own is not the loftiest prayer. A true appreciation of Fatherhood always involves the idea of Brotherhood. As Jesus said, "I ascend to My Father, and your Father; and to My God and your God" (John 20:17).

> For what are men better than sheep or goats,
> That nourish a blind life in their veins,
> If, knowing God, they lift not hands in prayer
> Both for themselves and those who call them friend?

At the moments of conviction of sin we feel that we stand alone—no one has sinned as we; and we say: God be merciful to me, the sinner; I have sinned and perverted that which was right, and it profited me not. In hours of awful sorrow we feel that we stand alone. Grief has a marvelous power of isolation—lover and friend stand afar off as we cry, "My God, my God, why hast Thou forsaken me?" But in our normal experiences we realize that we are drops in a great ocean, members in one body, units in the multitude which no one can number, and who stand before the throne of Him that lives forever, saying, "Our Father."

The door is always open; and, as you enter it, be sure to say, *"Our* Father," by which you include not simply your own brothers and sisters after the flesh—your mother and father, your wife and children, and the immediate relationships of your home—but a great company which is beyond estimation. The soul that can say "Father" is always conscious of being part of a vast brotherhood and sisterhood. Yonder is a woman who once lived to tempt, but now with a broken heart, in her poor, ill-furnished, dilapidated room, she is coming back to God, with words of penitence and contrition on her lips: is she included? Yes—*"our."* Yonder is a poor slave, whose flesh is quivering from the lash, and who, not noticed by man, is turning in his despair to God: is he included? Yes—*"our."* And yonder is a man who has always misunderstood and suspected you, has put unkind constructions upon your actions and words, and has imputed motives to you that you altogether repudiate: is he included? Yes—*"our."* Again, yonder is a man whom you have been accustomed to look upon as a heretic, because he does not exactly pronounce your Shibboleth, though he holds the Deity and saving work of our Lord: is he included? Yes—*"our."*

(4) *The True Standpoint of Prayer is the Honor and Glory of God.* If we take away the invocation and doxology, this prayer consists of seven petitions. The first three concern God—the hallowing of His Name; the coming of His Kingdom; the doing of His will. In this our Lord Jesus could join with His disciples. Then comes the single petition for daily bread. In this, again, our Lord could join His voice with ours. Indeed, the whole unfallen animal creation, and all holy beings throughout the universe, may in their measure add their volume of prayer that God would supply them with the sustenance they need. But, in the last three, prayers are enumerated for forgiveness, aid against temptation, and deliverance from evil, which are only applicable for ourselves as fallen creatures.

If you desire to pray aright, enter your closet, where God awaits you, kneel quietly before you attempt to address Him, that you may realize His presence, and the sights and scenes of earth cease to distract. Though it may take many minutes before the silt drops to the bottom and leaves the stream of your soul flowing pure and clear, the waiting will not be lost time; it is only thus that the blue heaven will be mirrored in the calm surface of your soul. The next step is to unite yourself with God's mighty purpose. Do not, in the first instance, ask what you want for yourself. Compel the intruding crowd of daily need and want to remain outside the fence with which you surround the base of the mountain of prayer, and go up alone to meet God, desiring to look at the needs of the world and at your own little life as subordinate to all that will make Him loved, honored, and adored. Put God's interests before your own. Enthrone God in your thoughts and petitions. Put first things first. Go forth and stand beneath the stars and count their number; mark their mighty orbits; realize the immensity of the sweep of God's movements—do this before you begin to count the glowworms at your foot, or the fireflies that fly around you in the dark.

On a campaign, a true soldier is more eager for the victory of the whole army than he is mindful of his own safety; his first thought is of his country's welfare; and he only puts in a plea for himself that he may better serve the interests of his fatherland. At first, this seems to be an impossible ideal, but it is, nevertheless, a true one; and we shall come to stand upon this pinnacle, if we set our hearts to it, that our whole aim and purpose in this mortal life should be to secure that God's Name should be hallowed, His Kingdom come, and His will be done. When we have poured out our soul in petitions for these, we may begin to urge our own need of daily bread and deliverance from evil.

"OUR FATHER." The suppliant must recognize that there is a bond of nature between God and himself, such as exists between child and parent. This has only to be suggested for its importance to be recognized. A child has a peculiar claim on its father. "You brought me into existence; you gave me the nature I possess; you understand its movements, and yearnings, and instincts, by a quick sympathy; you are bound by the strongest reasons to give me that which you know I need. I am part of you; and therefore lay claim that, as you nourish and cherish yourself, so you should nourish and cherish me." No stranger can introduce such tones into his speech. He may plead the claims of his need, of humanity, of gratitude, of friendship; but he cannot speak from the platform of a common nature. Amid a crowd of statesmen, state officials, court functionaries, attached and devoted friends, stands a young and slender boy; but there is a tie between him and the monarch, who is the center of the glittering throng, which no other person, however noble, can claim; and his requests have, therefore, a deeper and more preemptory demand than those of others.

It is thus that Jesus teaches us we should pray. There must be an innerness, a filial confidence, an entrance into the heart of God, because He is your Father by adoption and grace. And when this is your feeling toward Him, He will reciprocate it. Nay, He does not wait for you to approach Him thus, He anticipates your coming. As Judah said of Jacob, we may say of God: "His life is bound up in the lad's life" (Gen. 44:30). Like as a father pitieth his children, He pities us (Ps. 103:13). He loves us not in a mass, but each alone. His family is not larger to Him than ours to us; and, as we have a niche for each individual child, so has God. We may refuse to trust Him, and to avail ourselves of His help, but we cannot alter those words of Jesus, "The Father Himself loveth you" (John 16:27).

Three Conditions to Obey
There are three conditions, in obedience to which we may realize that God is our Father. Of course, there is only one Only-Begotten Son—One only can spell His name with a capital S. All others are sons with a small s. There is an impassable gulf between the Divine Sonship and the human sonship, however high, and to whatever degree of nearness that sonship may be raised.

(1) We all of us believe, with the heathen, that we have sprung from God. This has been the cherished thought of humans in every age and in every religion. The word Jupiter is made up of the two words *Zeus* and *pater*, the heavenly father; and travel where you may, under every sky and amid people of every tongue, you always find that this is

their deepest thought—that there is an All-Father from whom man has sprung. But this is not the deepest relationship; and it is not by this track that you will come home to abide most nearly to the Father's heart.

(2) Then, also, the Jews ever cherished the special belief that their nation stood in a unique relationship to God as Father. "Surely," they cried, in hours when anxiety and distress lay heavy upon their land, "surely Thou art our Father; though Abraham be ignorant of us, and Israel acknowledge us not, surely Thou art our Father." There was a kind of national relationship, therefore, between God and the Jews. But we cannot claim to stand with them on that ground, and the Lord Jesus showed that this sacred covenant relationship has been forfeited by their sin. "If," said He, "God were your Father" (John 8:42), you would recognize Me—implying that they had no right to call God "Father," because they had broken the covenant tie. Therefore He came—and this is the very heart of Christianity—that He might, by the Holy Spirit, reproduce in His children His own nature and Spirit. It is only as we receive Him that we have the right to become children of God, even as we believe in His Name (John 1:12).

(3) The Apostle says distinctly, "Ye are all the children of God *by faith* in Christ Jesus. . . . and because ye are . . . God hath sent the Spirit of His Son into your hearts," whereby you may call Him "Abba, Father" (Gal. 3:26; 4:6). Moreover, in that remarkable Second Epistle of St. John the beloved Apostle says, and the words are very significant, "He that abideth in the teaching"—that is, of the Gospel—"the same hath both the Father and the Son" (2 John 9, ASV).

From all these and many similar references we may judge that though we may belong to God as His offspring, we can never enter into the closest relationship until we are united by faith to His Son, who was born of a human mother, died on the Cross, and has now carried our nature to the right hand of God. By His Spirit we receive that nature into our own, and are thus in living affinity with the Son of God, who said, "I ascend unto My Father and your Father, and to My God and your God" (John 20:17), as though He desired us to realize that by union with Him God became our Father in almost though not quite the same sense in which He is His own.

God's Name and Nature

"HALLOWED BE THY NAME" (Matt. 6:9). The Name of God is His nature—His attributes the various properties that go to make Him what He is; and when we ask that it should be hallowed we ask that all which obscures the character of God should be swept away as mists before the rosy light of dawn. We thank God for all that is known of His wonderful nature, for the message of nature, for the revelations given to seers and prophets, for the life and death of the Son, for the gift of the Holy Spirit. But there are still great unexplored places. By reason of their sinful ignorance or superstition people have misunderstood and misrepresented the character of God; therefore we pray that in this world, and in all other worlds, His glorious personality may be understood, appreciated, and loved.

God's Kingdom

"THY KINGDOM COME" (Matt. 6:10). In one of those sublime flights with which the Epistles of St. Paul abound he tells us that the time is coming when the Son shall deliver up the Kingdom to God, even the Father, when He shall have abolished all rule, and authority, and power. From this we are at liberty to infer that the Kingdom was originally the Father's; that by man's sin and fall it has been alienated from His control, but that for purposes of recovery and redemption it has been handed over to the Well-Beloved Son. The Lord Jesus became incarnate for the purpose of regaining the Kingdom by His agony, blood, and tears; though it is not as yet His, it is being acquired; and it shall be His, and angel voices shall ring out the glad announcement that "the kingdoms of this world" have "become the kingdoms of our Lord and of His Christ" (Rev. 11:15). When, therefore, we pray Father, "Thy Kingdom come," we are asking that the complete victory of Jesus Christ may be hastened, that He may speedily triumph over all obstacles and enemies, that all tyranny may be extinguished, all corruption exposed; that truth may reign in government, art, and science; that trade may be free from chicanery and fraud; and that He may speedily send forth His angels to gather out of His Kingdom all things that offend, and them that do iniquity, destroying that last enemy, Death, and bringing in the golden age when all people shall know and love the Father, and become His obedient and loving children.

God's Will

"THY WILL BE DONE, AS IN HEAVEN, SO ON EARTH" (Matt. 6:10, ASV). There is a close connection between the *Name* and the *Will*. The *Name* is the Being of the Father, the nature of God, what He is in Himself; what He was, and is, and is to come. The *Will* is the energy of God, going forth perennially and omnipotently to the accomplishment of His own Divine and loving purpose. Clearly, then, the *Will* and the *Name* are but two sides of the same infinite, holy, and loving Being, who is Love. Therefore, whenever we say "Thy Will be done" we should begin by saying "Father"— "Our Father which art in heaven. . . . *Thy* Will be done, as in heaven, so on earth." It is because people catch up this petition suddenly, and without ascending to it through the regular gradients of the prayer, that it often seems so stern and terrible; but if only we can begin to say "My Father," then add "Our Father," and finally think of His nature, which, like some mighty ocean, full, deep, and placid, mirroring upon its surface the blue sky of eternity, is always sending forth tides of goodwill and peace in heaven and on earth, painting the tiniest flower that casts its shadow upon the lawn, and steering the mightiest world that rolls through space, always rising up in fountains of tenderness through heaven and earth—then we shall cease to utter this prayer as the address of a stoic or a cry of the grieved heart, or the reluctant expression of resignation on the part of a suffering soul, and it will become the anthem, the psalm of the whole life. "Father, Father, in all worlds, in all ages, and in my little life, let the energy of Thy Will work itself out to its fruition."

But is not God's Will always done, whether or not? Can

anyone resist it? Can any angel or demon overthrow it? Is it of use, is it wise, does it serve any purpose, to be ever saying, "Thy Will be done"? Surely it will be done, come what may. "He doeth according to His Will in the army of heaven and among the inhabitants of the earth, and none can stay His hand or say unto Him, What doest Thou?" (Dan. 4:35) Yes; but are you quite sure that God's *best* Will is always done? One is quite prepared to admit that generally, and on the whole, God's Will is done, but is His best Will done? The Royal Will may be done, but is the Father's Will done? And is not that the great difficulty in our world, that God's Will is resisted, while something which is second or third best is substituted? The failure between God's best and the best which becomes possible and practical through our resistance is that which brings discomfort, sorrow, friction, and pain into our lives. But if from today we would say "Heavenly Father, let Thy Will be wrought perfectly," Heaven would descend to brood in our breasts, and Paradise would come again to earth.

How many weary faces there are, tired and broken hearts, lives that have not fulfilled their full purpose and promise; and is not this because, though God has been working upon them for many years, yet He has met with so much tough resistance and obstinacy that He has not been able to realize His cherished plan? If only we would let the Father have His Will with us, to what a height of blessedness, and peace, and strength, might we not come. Young men and women, if, before you take the false and rash step—before you have allowed your own passions and desires to dictate your life-course—you would only let God mold you from the very outset, what fitness there would be in that prayer: Let Thy Will, the best Will, the Father's Will, be done, as it is done in heaven.

Our Daily Bread

"GIVE US THIS DAY OUR DAILY BREAD" (Matt. 6:11). In the Greek language there are two words for bread—first, *cytos* (corn bread). This, however, is not the word used by our Lord, but another, *artos*, which is a wider word, standing for food. Our Lord knew that this prayer of His was to be worldwide in its use, and, therefore, selected a term which would cover equally the rice of the Hindu, the blubber of the Eskimo, the macaroni of the Italian, and the oatmeal of the Scot—a general word standing for food. As He bids us to offer this prayer several things are suggested.

These words suggest great rest of heart about daily supplies, because, if Jesus Christ taught us to pray for daily bread, He implied that we had only to use the laws of prayer and labor, and God would supply all our need. He would never have put into our lips a prayer which was not in line with the thought and purpose of His Father. I know not what the anxieties of your life may be—about your health, or investments, or situation—but I do assure you that since Jesus Christ has put this prayer into your lips, it is already a pledge on God's part that He will feed you with convenient food, and supply your body with all that it requires, for its daily needs. "A body Thou hast prepared for me; and since Thou hast implanted its daily recurring appetites, Thou art surely responsible for their necessary satisfaction."

It is possible, of course, to indicate many people—perhaps God's children—who are suffering from hunger and privation. How is it that their food is so scanty and inconstant? I reply, May there not be some lack in their faith, and may it not be that they *have not* because they *ask not*, or because they do not exercise definite faith in God? God loves to give, not bread alone, but fish. "They saw a fire . . . and fish laid thereon and bread" (John 21:9). Not necessaries only, but luxuries.

There is many a pang of hunger in human nature which remains after the physical deprivation and want have been met. In fact, a good many would find it comparatively easy to suffer physical hunger if they were delivered from suffering other unsatisfied appetites of the nature, which are always crying out, "Give, give." For instance, how many of us are hungering for *human love*, sometimes to the point of absolute starvation, looking eagerly for one tiny crumb to fall from a beloved hand, or from the banquet on which others feast so bountifully? Are there not some whose minds are voracious for *truth*? They desire to understand mysteries that baffle; to penetrate the heavy mist that veils the eternal mountains. Theirs is a spirit of a John Foster, who would talk with rapture of the revelations that waited on the other side of death.

Besides these, are there not some whose deepest nature cries out for God; for that Bread of Life that comes down from heaven; for more of the indwelling and the nourishment of His character? These are they who have entered into the meaning of the Saviour's own words: "Man shall not live by bread alone, but by every word that proceedeth out of the mouth of God" (Matt. 4:4).

When, therefore, we kneel before God in prayer and utter this petition, with some the words mean: Give us today some gleams of human love, some sign that our work is appreciated, and is telling upon others for good; truth upon which our minds may feed and grow strong, for they that know God are strong and do exploits; and, above all, feed our spirits with Thyself, for Thou hast implanted an appetite after the unseen and eternal, which can never be met by anything which is merely transient and temporal.

When we say, "Give us, graciously and freely, bread for today," do we not imply that all good and perfect gratification must come from God? Do you not like to emphasize that word *give*? Do you not think that is a truer conception of life than that we must snatch at any gratification that is within our reach? How often we are tempted to make a raid on what promises to appease the yearnings of our affection; to extract some word of appreciation; to press into precincts where we have no right to stand, and to ask people for gifts which they have no right to bestow. Yet, when we say this prayer from our hearts as Jesus meant us to say it, we look up to God's face and say: "Father, Thou madest our frame, Thou understandest its appetites; Thou art well acquainted with all the yearnings, hopes, and fears that pass through our nature, and I, Thy child, will take satisfaction from no hand but Thine; give me what I really need for all the necessary appetites of today." Then wait expectantly before God, till there be some communication of Himself, some arrangement of His providence, some sending of a Titus, or the advent of a letter, or telegram, or parcel, the glint of some new truth, or a text from the Bible, or a paragraph in a biography—something in which God shall Himself give us our daily bread.

Does your life seem almost intolerable in its penury, poverty, and precariousness of subsistence? Then turn to the Father and say: "I am determined to wait on Thee all day; not turning the stones into bread by any alienation of power or talent with which I am endued, but prepared to wait until Thou shalt open Thine hand and satisfy my need, or send Thine angels to minister."

Surely God would never have placed within the scope of human nature any hunger, which is in itself natural and innocent, without pledging Himself at the same time to give it due nourishment and support. Besides, look into nature. The birds of the forest seek food which has been stored for them in the berries of the autumn; the fish, as they flash from the lake, find the fly provided for them; the young lions, as they roar through the forest and seek their meat from God, find that He opens His hand and gives it. And it is impossible to suppose that He will starve those appetites which He has implanted. You may have to hunger a little in order that more of the evil in your appetite may be eliminated, that its passion may die down, that what is wrong may be extracted; but the desire itself, insofar as it is part of the nature which He has given, will surely be gratified somehow, somewhen. Wait on the Lord, therefore, and be of good courage; no good thing will He withhold from them that walk uprightly (Ps. 84:11).

No one has a right to utter that prayer unless he is prepared, so far as He can, to answer it. Obviously it demands that he should be prepared to work for his living; that he should go forth in the morning and toil through the hours of the busy day, coming back weary at night. It implies that he should put his shoulder to the wheel. It also implies that he should not earn for himself alone, but for others; and that, insofar as in him lies, he should minister to their hunger. A man has no right to pray this who is not also prepared to open his wallet, and when there is really need for bread, to give it.

But in a deeper sense a similar thought holds true. We

say that hunger is possible for affection, for appreciation, for truth, for God; and when we say, "Give us this day *our* daily bread," we really include all lonely hearts, all who weary for a smile, all who are pining for love, all who are seeking for truth, all who want God; and taking your stand among this ragged, eager, hungry crowd, you, as their spokesman, say: "Give all such their daily bread."

Does it not mean, also, that if you know some weary soul wanting a kindly word you should speak it? That, if you know of one who is famishing for human love, you should, if possible, pass some on? That, if there are within your reach those who need the truth of God, and you can supply it, it should not be lacking? That, if there are any who need that impulse of new vigor which comes from the touch of a spiritual person, to reinvigorate, reanimate, and reinspire, none of these should be wanting?

Answer this prayer so far as you may; and just because the world is so hungry, and weary, and famishing, go forth and be its breadwinners and its breadgivers. As far as you can, help to alleviate the despair and hopelessness, the misery and the sin of people, by passing on the Bread of God, the Bread of Life, the Bread of Love, the Bread of Hope, upon which you feed. Share your last crust with another. If you get a glint of light, flash it on. If you get a new truth, communicate it. If you get a baptism of the Holy Spirit, never rest until others rejoice in it too.

Our Debts and Our Debtors

"AND FORGIVE US OUR DEBTS, AS WE FORGIVE OUR DEBTORS" (Matt. 6:12). Every word in this prayer deserves our thought. One might dwell at length on the conjunction *"and,"* for it is remarkable that by it this petition is conjoined to that for daily bread; these only of all the petitions in this prayer are linked together. "Give us this day our daily bread, and forgive us our debts, as we forgive our debtors."

The conclusion is an obvious one—that we need forgiveness as often as we need our daily bread; that our need for forgiveness is as urgent as our need for daily food; and that the forgiveness of God is as lavish as His giving is, which stores the cornfields with the golden grain, and spreads so richly the repast of fruits and vegetables for human need.

Do you recognize this? Are you conscious of this deep need for forgiveness? Do you experience cravings for it—insatiable as your cravings of hunger for food? Are you aware that in God's sight your soul is starving, just because you have not learned to know your own deep need? The drug of worldly engagement has made you oblivious to the hunger of your spirit; but if you truly knew yourself you would never lift your heart to thank God for your food without pleading for forgiveness; and there would be the recurrent sense, that even in your happiest, holiest days there are things that need to be forgiven, the blood needs to be applied, the sense of God needs to spread over your soul. "Give me daily bread—I want that; but as often as I need it, grant forgiveness too."

The Greek word used by Luke, and translated *trespasses* (Matt. 6:14), means to *miss the mark.* Every one of us aims, as we hope truly, at the mark, but we miss it. We come back like the prodigal, saying, "Father, I have missed the mark. I meant to be a good and holy and dutiful son; I aimed at it in my early life, but as the years have passed I have missed it."

But in Matthew our Lord sets forth another thought—*that sin is debt,* that it is a failure to pay our dues. If the one is the positive, this is the negative side. Trespass is positive, debt negative. "We have done the things we ought not," is trespass; "we have not done the things that we ought," is debt.

Every relationship means responsibility. Every tie by which we are bound to other men and women has its obligation, and there are times when the sense of our debts overwhelms us. Who is there of the holiest and best among us that is not sometimes absolutely overwhelmed by the sense of the obligations which have not been discharged, of the debts which remained unpaid? There is not a single person living who has ever perfectly discharged his debts to other souls, and certainly none who has discharged them to the Almighty. Warning bells are sometimes so constructed that they move with every movement of the waves; some are therefore perpetually tolling, as every surge causes them to yield their monotonous note. Do you not realize that conscience is always tolling the bell of ought, of obligation, of dues not realized?

Forgiveness in the old Anglo-Saxon is *forthgiving*. It is what you give forth; what you give away; which passes from your hand. The Greek word is to remit, to cancel, to dismiss—so that what has existed as an obligation ceases to be such. Our Lord then teaches us to ask that God would so remit what has been wrong, so cancel what has been left unpaid, that though in a sense we shall never be able to make right what is wrong to our fellows, yet the guilt of it will no longer accrue to us. When a person is truly forgiven he may claim not only that the guilt will pass off his own soul, but that God's repairing hand will make right what has been left wrong, adjusting his undischarged obligations, so that those souls which have been wronged by him may, by God's good hand, somehow be compensated. Sin is debt; but there is forgiving, remission, the putting absolutely away. The fact that our Lord taught us to use this prayer proves that we may count on an answer, because He was the Lamb slain before the foundation of the world, and He has taken away its sin.

When God says *forgiven*, He also says *restored*; and when a soul looks wistfully at those whom it has wronged, and asks, "How about these?" God seems to say, "I know the debt incurred; I have forgiven thee, and I will now repair." Then the blessed Spirit of God reaches out to the souls whom we have wronged; by a touch He transmutes the wrong, and into the wound pours the oil and balm. When a child of God understands that, his heart becomes very pitiful; having felt the agony of his own indebtedness and the joy of forgiveness, he begins to look around, and, instead of saying *me*, he says *our*. He thinks of his dear ones, and pleads, like Job, each morning, "Forgive the sins of my home." He thinks of the neighborhood in which he dwells, and says, "O my God, I pray for these men and women around me, that Thou would forgive them." Then, as a priest, he takes the whole world into his embrace and pleads, "O God, for the sake of Thy Son, forgive them; they

115

know not what they do." The answer to that prayer is a Pentecost in which people are stabbed to the heart and led to cry for the mercy which God longs to show.

"AND LEAD US NOT INTO TEMPTATION, BUT DELIVER US FROM EVIL" (Matt. 6:13). We who are true children of God recognize our spiritual weakness, so we pray for deliverance from temptation to do evil. It is right and necessary to pray for protection from wrongdoing. "Lead us not into temptation" does not mean that God tempts His children (James 1:13-17). In this petition we are asking God to guide us so that we will not get out of His will and get involved in a situation of tempting God so that He will be asked to miraculously rescue us (Matt. 4:5-7).

God's Kingdom, Power, and Glory

"THINE IS THE KINGDOM, AND THE POWER, AND THE GLORY FOREVER. AMEN" (Matt. 6:13). The authenticity and validity of this Doxology is questioned. Many ancient authorities, however, include it, and it does seem a natural termination for this glorious prayer. The Kingdom is God's, though His claims are set at nought by people who say, "Let us break [His] bands asunder and cast away [His] cords from us" (Ps. 2:3). Yet God is King. I never shall forget that archway in Damascus which for centuries has looked down upon the misrule of the Turk, but which bears the deep-cut inscription, "Thy Kingdom, O Christ, is an everlasting Kingdom." Let us repeat it again and again, *"Thine is the Kingdom."*

"Thine is . . . the Power." He has the power to set up His Kingdom to overcome evil with good, hate with love, and darkness with light. Whatever ideals He may have raised in the heart or for the world, to God belongs enough power to make them facts in experience.

"Thine is . . . the glory." This is the consummation of all. We are told that in the campaign of the great Napoleon, when his soldiers were being mown down in battle, they would turn toward him waving their hands, and with their last gasps of breath cry, *"Vive l'Empereur!"* So in life and death we cry, "Glory to God in the highest." This the climax of every prayer, the passion of life and death.

Forgive People, or Remain Unforgiven by God

Our Lord returns (Matt. 6:14) to one clause in the prayer that emphasizes the thought which was already implicated in the structure of the fifth position when He told us that in asking for forgiveness of our debts, we must always say, "As we forgive our debtors." Notice the alteration made in the American Standard Version; it is not "As we forgive," but *"As we also have forgiven"* (Matt. 6:12, ASV). This carries us back, of course, to 5:24, where we are told to leave our gift at the altar, and to be reconciled to our brother before we offer our gift.

Our Lord does not mean, of course, that God's forgiveness is measured by our own, or that our forgiveness is the cause of God's. Neither of these is the true rendering of this clause, but that God does not forgive an unforgiving spirit. The fact is that the only sure index that our contrition and penitence are genuine is that we forgive. If we do not forgive, if our heart does not go out in pity and forgiving love, it proves that we must have been mistaken about ourselves, and have never attained that true position of soul before God in which He is able to forgive.

Have you not noticed this in your life, that after the consciousness of forgiveness through the Blood of the Atonement, which is not mentioned here, but implied, that the joy of forgiveness sometimes dies off your soul, and you question whether it was not a phantom, a bright and blessed dream? You wonder whether the words of absolution were really spoken, and wearily resume your burden. You cannot tell why it is, but it seems as though your sin had come back again on you. Let me explain! In our Lord's parable a king forgave a man who owed ten thousand talents, and the poor debtor was glad; but leaving his presence he met a debtor of his own who owed him two hundred pence. This man he took by the throat, saying, "Pay me what thou owest." The result was that he was brought back to the king, and his pardon cancelled, so that he again stood liable for the ten thousand talents (Matt. 18:23-35). Why? Because he was unforgiving, and an unforgiving person loses the sense of God's forgiveness. The reason, then, why you have lost the sense of forgiveness is probably because you have stood upon your rights, have insisted upon other people doing to you what you have failed to do to God, and because you have been deficient in the forgiveness that you have sought. It is only when we have learned to forgive that the Spirit of God maintains in our hearts the blessed consciousness of forgiveness.

How is it with you? Do you forgive? Or are there men and women that you obdurately refuse to forgive? If there are, it shows that your own soul is not right before God. Your love to God is gauged by your love to people; your relationship to God is indicated by your relationship to your fellows. The one who does not love the brother whom he has seen cannot love the God whom he has not seen (1 John 4:20). Discover where you are today. If there are men and women in your life that you refuse to pray for and forgive, know that your heart is wrong with God. Do the *first* thing, begin to pray for them, and say, "Forgive *us*, that person who has hurt me, that one who has wronged me; he needs forgiveness, but I need it equally. We are both in the wrong; I might have made it easier for him to do right than I have done." Begin with prayer. That is the first step; compel yourself to pray, "Forgive us both." *Secondly*, ask for the opportunity to meet him. *Thirdly*, claim that when you meet there may be in you the royalty of God's grace, that you may bear yourself with that rare, gracious love which covers the multitude of sins (1 Peter 4:8). Be willing that through your lips God's pitying mercy may pass forth in words of human kindness.

May God, for the sake of Christ, cancel our indebtedness, and mercifully go over the wrongs we have done to others and repair them. Then, if He gives us the opportunity, may we use it to act justly, kindly, lovingly, nobly, generously, toward those whom we have wronged.

Dear God, forgive us our debts, and help us to forgive those who are indebted to us!

CHAPTER FIFTEEN

THE DISCIPLES' USE OF MONEY

(Matt. 6:19-21, 24)*

There are two things which distort our eyesight—that is, which hinder the pure intention of the soul: the one is the temptation of the prosperous and well-to-do; the other of the poor, reminding us of the seed that was sown among the thorns. This "is he that heareth the Word, and the care of this world [this is the temptation of the poor and struggling], and the deceitfulness of riches [this is the temptation of those who are endeavoring or beginning to obtain property], choke the Word, and he becometh unfruitful" (Matt. 13:22).

It is of the temptations which accrue in dealing with money that we have now to speak. Our message is to those who, to use the words of the Apostle, are "minded to be rich" (ASV). These are they who "fall into temptation and a snare, and into many foolish and hurtful lusts, which drown men in destruction and perdition" (1 Tim. 6:9).

The Uncertainty of Riches

Our Lord, first, alludes to the ephemeral and destructible character of earthly riches. Oriental wealth consisted largely of magnificently embroidered dresses; and in a land where

---

*Matthew 6:16-18 is covered in Chapter 13.

there were no banks (in our sense of the term), coins would be buried in the earth—often, as in the case of Achan, in a hole dug inside the house (Josh. 7:21). We remember also the parable of our Lord about hidden treasure in a field (Matt. 13:44), the owner of which had no idea of the buried wealth that lay beneath the surface of the soil, until his plow came into collision with it, and the metallic ring indicated that he should stop his oxen in order to disentomb the jar of coins, hidden when an invasion swept the country, and which the proprietor never returned to claim.

Our Lord reminds His hearers that moth or rust will destroy all their earthly treasures, and that thieves may at any moment break through the slight clay walls of their homes and carry off their hoarded stores. Surely His words are an extended reference to Death, that "crowned and sceptered thief," who shall one day dig through the clay walls of our mortal house, and take from us the raiment in which we have been attired, the wealth we may have amassed, the shares that stand in our name, the lands that we have purchased, sending us forth naked and despoiled, stripped of everything, into a world where we may land as paupers, if we have failed to lay up treasure there.

Our Lord could not for a moment have meant to denounce every kind of saving. For instance, the Apostle Paul enjoins on parents the duty of laying up for their children (2 Cor. 12:14). It is surely right for us to take advantage of the laws of savings and life insurance that we may make a reasonable and moderate provision against old age, and especially that we should, by a small annual payment, secure for those who may survive us some sort of income. I seriously think that all young men and women should, in the early years of their lives, commence to pay into one of our large insurance offices, so that at the age of fifty-five, or sixty, a sum may be forthcoming which will be of use to them in their declining years—the same sum being paid to mother, wife, or sister, in case of their premature death; and I cannot for a moment believe that the spirit or letter of our Lord's words contradict this item of economics.

It seems also certain that there is nothing in these words of the Master to prohibit the setting apart of a certain sum as capital, which may be used for the development of business, and therefore in the employment of a large number of workers. Nothing seems to me more beneficent than that a manufacturer should add to his capital, and therefore to his machinery and yearly output, for all this means the widening of his influence and the provision of work to larger numbers of men, women, girls, and lads—the more especially if he contributes to the building up of some garden city, free from the facilities of drink, free from the confinement of the great city, free from the vices which are incident to every great aggregation of humanity, where every home is within sight of trees and flowers, where every working person has his plot of land, and where the children breathe fresh health-giving air.

But neither of these methods of laying aside money is contrary to our Lord's injunction, "Lay not up for yourselves treasures upon earth" (Matt. 6:19). What He forbids is amassing money, not for the use we make of it, not for securing our loved ones from anxiety, but for its own sake, to such an extent that the endeavor to hoard engrosses affections which ought to be fixed on nobler and diviner things, and leads to concentrating one's whole being on the growing balance in the bank or the increase of real estate. In the judgment of eternity it is unworthy of an immortal being to imperil his highest interests, his vision of God, his spiritual power, his peace and blessedness, for things which are so lightly held and easily lost as riches. Granted, most things for which people strive are no longer destroyed by moth and rust, or stolen by thieves, yet the uncertainty of riches is proverbial; at any moment they may take wings and fly away. A panic on the Stock Exchange, depreciation in the value of securities, a new invention, the diversion of trade from one port to another, or the competition of a foreigner, may in a short time cause the carefully hoarded winnings of our lifetime to crumble like the Venice Campanile [an ill-fated bell tower].

The Danger in Amassing Riches
Our Lord might with good reason have denounced the practice of laying up treasure because of the temptation which the desire to

121

gain it involves. If a young man possesses the one intention of making a fortune as quickly as he can, he is almost sure to begin making it according to the maxims and practices which prevail in the world around him. From afar he sees the goal that beckons, and he is tempted to take the shortest cut to reach it, along a road strewn thick with lies and roguery, with lost reputations and blasted characters. That road is taken by myriads in the mad rush to become rich, irrespective of the misery which may be involved to others, and the injury which is being wrought on themselves. Well did our Lord describe riches as "the unrighteous mammon" (Luke 16:11). Therefore, with the utmost urgency one would reiterate to all who are commencing to earn a living, in the words with which the great Apostle to the Gentiles closed one of the last Epistles: "Charge them that are rich in this present world, that they be not highminded, nor have their hope set on the uncertainty of riches, but on God, who giveth us richly all things to enjoy" (1 Tim. 6:17, ASV).

Five Tests of One's Attitude toward Money

Let us turn now to the reasons which our Lord adduces for His urgent prohibition against the amassing of treasure by His disciples.

First, *the hoarding of money induces an inordinate love for it.* "Where thy treasure is, there will thy heart be also" (Matt. 6:21). There is a strong temptation to the most devout man who begins his life consecrated to God and to the best service of his fellows, when he sees money beginning to accumulate in his possession, to be attracted from the main object of life to his rising pile. Let young businessmen who bear the name of Christ test themselves, and ask whether their hearts are not being insensibly stolen away. They may not be aware of what is happening. Gray hairs may be becoming plentifully strewn upon their heads without their knowing it. The fascination of money is one of the strongest lures in the whole world. It is almost impossible to handle it, whether the money has come down as an inheritance from the past, or has been gained by successful trading in the present, without coming to like it for its own sake, to congratulate oneself when it increases, and to scheme for its further accumulation. Thus the heart becomes unconsciously bound by ever-tightening chains, as a balloon filled with light gas, and meant to hold commerce with the clouds, chafes at the strong hawsers by which it is held to the earth.

It is not difficult for onlookers to discern the process by which the heart is being weaned away from the Unseen and the Eternal to the temporal and transient. There is a slackening of interest in religious worship and Christian service; an absorption amid the home circle which shows that the heart is no longer there; a reluctance to part with money that once used to be freely given for home and foreign missions. It becomes increasingly difficult to engage the attention in anything which involves the diversion of time or thought from the bank, the factory, or the store. The process is very subtle; but, on the comparison of years, those who love the tempted and notice his fascinated nature, shake their heads gravely as they realize that the heart is being betrayed to its ruin, and that another life will soon be cast beneath the wheels of the terrible Juggernaut Car of worldly ambition and success.

There are various tests by which we may become aware whether this parasite is wrapping itself around us. Let us dare to question our hearts, and ask God to search them by His Holy Spirit. These five will suffice:

(1) Do we find our mind going toward the little store of money which we have made, with a considerable amount of complacency, casting up again and again its amount, and calculating how much more may be added in the course of another year? When we are sleepless at night, or sit back in the corner of our railway carriage, do we find ourselves habitually going in the one direction of that growing competence? If so, is it not clear that our heart is being fascinated and attracted?

(2) Does the thought constantly intrude in our mind that there is now less likelihood than ever of our spending the end of our days in a poorhouse, or being dependent upon others, even upon God Himself? Do we look back upon the days of early manhood and compare them with the present,

feeling that we are becoming independent? Is our trust in God less complete than it used to be? Is there not danger, therefore, of our weak and deceitful heart trusting in these uncertain riches, and being robbed of that simple faith which used to be the charm of earlier days, when we were content to do His work and trust Him for all that was necessary?

(3) Do we envy others who are making money more rapidly than we are, and count ourselves ill-used because we cannot keep pace with them?

(4) Do we look at every service we perform—at our extending knowledge of people, at every new piece of information that we gather—in the light of its monetary advantage?

(5) Is it our habit to measure the gains of the year simply by what we have made, with no reference to what we are? Do we review the money we have accumulated, rather than the good we have done?

It becomes us to ask ourselves such questions as these reverently, as in the sight of God, and thoughtfully for our own highest interests, for they will reveal to us almost certainly whether the slow poison of an absorbing love of money may not be stealing through our heart, robbing it of its noblest attributes. It is a terrible thing for us to love gold for its own sake, rather than for the use that we may make of it, because the heart is likely to become like that which it loves. Not only is the heart buried in the place where the treasure is, but the heart becomes like the treasure. Ossification is a terrible physical disease, when the heart turns to a hard, bony substance; but it has a spiritual counterpart for those whose love for gold shrivels the heart into something nearly as hard as metal.

How Money Can Blind One to Spiritual Light

It is not necessary for us to dwell at length on the second reason which our Lord adduces against treasuring our treasures, namely, that *hoarding money diverts the pure intention of the soul and blinds all spiritual light*. We all know that faith is only possible for the pure heart. The faculty of spiritual vision and receptivity depends upon the simplicity and integrity of one's moral life. When, therefore, the heart is filled with thoughts of its earthly riches, it becomes gross and insensible to the spiritual and eternal realm. Things of God fade from the vision, the love of God declines from the heart, the soul is no longer single in its purpose, the eye becomes dim, the spiritual force abated, moral paralysis sets in, and the whole body becomes full of darkness, under the cover of which evil things creep forth. Oh, do not let your spiritual eyes become dazzled by the glitter of this world's goods, lest you be unable, like Bunyan's man with the muckrake, to see the angel who, with golden crown in hand, waits to bless you. Instead of crouching over your heap of transient treasure, rise to your full stature, and claim the crown that fadeth not away! (1 Peter 5:4)

How Money Can Enslave

The third reason that our Lord adduces is that *hoarding money finally enslaves.* He says that "No man can serve two masters, for either he will hate the one and love the other, or else he will hold to the one and despise the other. Ye cannot serve God and Mammon" (Matt. 6:24). He employs two significant words—the one, *Mammon* (an old Chaldean word for the god of wealth); the other, *to serve,* the subjection of a slave to the caprice of an owner. Our Lord puts in juxtaposition the two masters—God the Beneficent Father, and Mammon the god of wealth, and says everyone must choose between them. Whichever you elect to serve will become the supreme dominating force in your life, giving you no option, except the obedience of a slave.

Notice then the peril of a Christian who is falling under the sway of covetousness which the Apostle calls idolatry (Eph. 5:5; Col. 3:5). At the end of the process, be it longer or shorter, he will renounce entirely the service of God, and become a slave of money-making. The slightest acquaintance with commercial circles will give evidence of the tyranny of Mammon, which compels its abject slaves to toil day and night, demands the sacrifice of love and health, of home enjoyments and natural pleasures, insists that every interest shall be subordinate to its all-consuming service, and at the end of life casts its victims, bankrupt and penniless, upon the shores of eternity. Drink itself, which strips people of everything worth living for, is not more to be dreaded.

How Money Should Be Handled

What then is the alternative to this prohibited hoarding of money? Are we to give away promiscuously and to everyone that asks? I confess I have no faith in this indiscriminate giving which demoralizes the one who gives and him who receives; which creates a plentiful harvest of loafers and ne'er-do-wells, to the detriment of the thrifty and industrious poor, and which satisfies the sentiment of pity by a lazy dole, when it ought to set itself to a radical amelioration of the suppliant beggar. It is comparatively fruitless to give a meal here and there, without endeavoring, by practical sympathy and helping hand, to assist families by teaching them to help themselves. This is what is needed; and to put one individual, or houseful, in the way of standing upon their own feet and securing their own livelihood, is immensely more important than to furnish temporary relief, that supplies the need of today, but makes no permanent alteration in the circumstances of tomorrow or of the future. It is much more difficult to use our money thoughtfully and thriftily to help others than to place half a crown or a sovereign in their hands. Here, for instance, is a poor woman, whose case appeals to your sympathy. It is, of course, quite easy to give her a few shillings and to dismiss her from your mind, but the noblest thing would be to secure her a sewing machine or a mangle, thus furnishing her with an opportunity for self-help. It is quite as important not to give money indiscriminately as it is not to hoard. The ideal method of life is to *use* what you have to help others, to regard your possession of money as a stewardship for the welfare of the world, and to consider yourself a trustee for some who need. Instead of letting your dresses hang in the wardrobe, give them to the respectable poor whose own are threadbare, that they may be able to occupy suitably the position on which their livelihood depends. This is the best way of keeping them free from moth. Whatever you have in the way of books, recreation, spare rooms, elegantly furnished homes, look upon them all as so many opportunities of helping and blessing others.

If you are in business, at the end of the year put aside what is needed for the maintenance of your family in the position to which God has called them; next, put aside what may be required for the development of your business; third, be sure that by a system of life insurance you are providing for the failure of old age; but when all this is done, look upon the remainder as God's, to be used for Him. Never give God less than a tenth, but give Him as much more as possible. If you have money by inheritance, you have no right to give that away or squander it; but pass it down as you received it, always considering, if you will, that the interest is God's, awaiting your administration as His steward and trustee.

Let every Christian adopt the principle of giving a certain proportion of his income to the cause of Christ, and whenever the fascination of money begins to assert itself, instantly make a handsome donation to some needy cause. Every time the temptation comes to look at money from a selfish standpoint, meet it by saying to God, "I thank Thee that Thou hast given me these things richly to enjoy, and desire wisdom and grace to use them for Thee and Thine."

What will be the result of a spiritual attitude like this? Ah, the full blessedness cannot be put in words—but this you will find: you will have treasure in heaven, for what you invest in ministering to others is capital laid up in God's Bank, the interest of which will always be accruing to you. I have a very distinct belief that actual interest comes from money which is being invested in doing good; and at last those we have helped will welcome us into the eternal mansions (Luke 16:9). Moreover, your heart will be increasingly fixed where your treasure is, in the Unseen and the Eternal. Your eye will be single, your life harmonious, your hold upon earthly things slender, your love for your Master, Christ, becoming a passion. Ultimately you will find that the yearning which you used to have for selfish satisfaction and comfort will pass away, as the blessing of Him that was ready to perish falls upon your head, and the thanks of the widow and orphan anticipate the "Well done!" of your Lord.

CHAPTER SIXTEEN

THE INTENTION OF THE SOUL

(Matt. 6:22-23)

The eyes form the most striking and important feature in the face. Blue as the azure of heaven, brown as hazel, or black as jet, they give expression and beauty to the countenance, fill with tears of pity, sparkle with the radiance of affection, and flash with the fire of anger. By the eyes we are able, therefore, to discern much of the thoughts and intents of one's heart.

Eyes are also urgently needed to enable us to do the work of life. It is by our eyes that we see to do our work, discover the paths in which we must tread, and look upon the faces of our friends, and the beauty of God's Creation. Each time we see a blind person, or pass institutions devoted for the recovery of sight, let us lift up our hearts to thank God for the priceless boon of sight.

It is interesting to notice the comparison which our Lord employs. He speaks of "the eye" as "the light of the body" (Matt. 6:22); in other places, the same Greek word is rendered "lamp," or "candle." In a previous chapter we discover the same expression: "Neither do men light a candle and put it under a bushel" (Matt. 5:15). The same word is used by Luke: "Let your loins be girded about, and your lights burning" (Luke 12:35). It is the word by which John the Baptist is designated: "He was a burning and a shining

128

light" (John 5:35), in contradistinction to the other term, applied to our Lord alone: "That was the true Light which lighteth every man that cometh into the world" (John 1:9). The ministry of John was the lamp that lighted the steps of people until "the Sun of Righteousness [would] arise with healing in His wings" (Mal. 4:2). The eye, our Lord says, is the lamp of the house of the body. It is as though He thought of the eye as hanging in the vestibule of the palace of life, casting its rays outward to the busy thoroughfare, and inward to the recesses of the soul.

The Eye of the Soul

It is obvious that there must be something in our inner life that corresponds to the eye, for our Lord refers to the eye as the emblem and symbol of something within. He is not speaking of the eye of the body only, but of its correlative, the eye of the soul.

What is that inner eye? Some have supposed that it is the power of a concentrated affection, for truly love sheds a warm glow over all the furniture of the inner life as well as upon the great world without.

Others have affirmed that the intellect is the eye of the soul, by which we are able to behold the ordered process of the world, and to consider the processes of thought within us.

A truer conception of our Lord's meaning, however, will lead to the conclusion that the eye of the body corresponds to the inward intention and purpose of the soul.

If, for a moment, you will examine your inner life, descending to the profound depths that lie beneath the surface of your being, you will discover that there is one deep aim or purpose which is the real intention of your life. Deep down, below the play of emotion and intellect, and of engagement in various interests, there is one strong stream or current running perpetually through the dark ravines of your nature. It may be that you are hardly aware of it; your nearest and dearest friends do not realize it. You would be startled if it were stated in so many words, but it is nonetheless true, that there is a unity in each human character which God perceives. In each of us He can read a unity of purpose and a unity of will. This is the intention of the soul, and distinguishes each of us from everyone else.

The eye may of course be healthy or unhealthy. If healthy, a tiny curtain which hangs at the back of the organism is adjusted to receive the focused rays which come from external objects. On this tiny curtain is formed an inverted image of all things which are visible. If you look into the eye of another, and especially into the eye of a little babe, you will see the whole panorama of the world presented as in a movie. This curtain is perpetually being readjusted, so that the unblurred image of the outer world may be cast upon it. When we are traveling in a railway train it is probable that in a single hour the focus is altered thousands of times, for at every jolt and oscillation of the vehicle there must be a readjustment of the focus.

When the eye is in an unhealthy condition the image is doubled or blurred. There are several ways in which an eye may become "evil." To use a common expression, there may be the obliquity called a squint, such as disfigured the noble face of Edward Irving. Mrs. Oliphant tells us that as a babe he was laid in a wooden cradle, through a hole in which he was able to watch the light with one eye, while the other retained its usual straightforward direction. His eyes, therefore, were not parallel, and it was impossible to focus them upon a given object. Similarly one's soul's intention may be diverted from a single purpose in a double direction. We may pray with the object of gaining an answer from God, and at the same time of receiving credit from man. We may try to amass the treasures of this world, and at the same time be rich toward God. We may endeavor to serve two masters—God and Mammon. This is the counterpart in the spiritual life of a squint in the eye.

Another source of ill health with the eye is when the little vesicles which supply blood for the tiny curtain become overcharged so that it is impossible for the delicate nerves to adjust the lense, and the vision becomes blurred and indistinct.

Yet another source of the evil eye is when a film forms over the surface of the pupil, so that much of the light cannot enter.

In contradistinction to these evils, how good it is to have a clear eye with its distinct vision, and how much more good it is, when the purpose and intention of the soul is so undivided that the whole of life is illumined by the glow of a clear and beautiful light. All through this chapter (Matt. 6) our Lord is arguing against this double vision. He says, "Do not profess to belong to the Kingdom of Heaven while your hearts are buried in the earth; do not have two masters; do not be divided by anxious care; seek first the Kingdom of God." All through this chapter He is, in fact, bidding us to make our constant prayer the cry of the Psalmist, "Unite my heart to fear Thy Name" (Ps. 86:11). Our Lord sets His whole force against any duplication of character so inimitably described by John Bunyan, of Mr. Facing-Both-Ways, with one eye on heaven and another on earth, who sincerely professed one thing and sincerely did another, and from the inveteracy of his unreality was unable to see the contradiction of his life. "He tried to cheat both God and the Devil, and in reality he only cheated himself and his neighbors."

Different Kinds of People

There are three kinds of people. First, those who have no intention. Second, those who have a double intention. Third, those whose intention is pure and simple.

(1) SOME HAVE NO INTENTION. They live day by day without purpose; the eye of the mind is fixed definitely and intently upon nothing. They take each day as it comes, getting from it anything it may bring, doing the duty it demands; but their existence is from hand to mouth, haphazard, with no aim, no ambition, no godly purpose. They cannot say, with the Apostle, that they are leaving the things which are behind, and pressing forward to the things which are before, and this one thing they are ever engaged in doing (Phil. 3:13-14). It is quite true that in many cases there may be no great cause to be championed, no subjects to be explored, no object in making money, because already there is an ample competence. Some may read these words who are daughters in a wealthy home, or young men, the heirs of a considerable fortune, others peo-

ple in humble life who have no great need to look beyond the day or week with its ordinary routine; but even these should have a supreme purpose, to bring down the New Jerusalem out of heaven to establish the Kingdom of God among people, to hasten the coming of the day of Christ, or to be themselves purer and holier. To *become* should always be the supreme purpose and intention of the soul; to be a little more like Christ; to know and love Him better; to be able to shed more of His sweetness and strength upon others. There is no life so contained within the high walls of circumstances which may not reach up toward the profound light of the azure sky that arches above.

Do not be content to drift through life; do not be satisfied to be a piece of driftwood, swept to and fro by the ebb and flow of the stream; do not be a creature of circumstance; because it is certain that if you are not living with a Divine purpose for God and eternity, you are certainly living for yourself, for your ease, or your indolent enjoyment, or to get through the years with as little fret and friction as possible, which, at the heart of it, and in such a world as this, so abject and needy, is undiluted selfishness. To have no purpose is to have the worst purpose; to have no ambition is to be living for self; to have no intention is to be drifting along the broad road in company with the many that go in thereat to their own destruction (Matt. 7:13).

(2) SOME HAVE A DOUBLE INTENTION. They have heard the call of Christ and have received the seed of the Kingdom; but as soon as it reached their hearts, two strong competitors endeavored to share with it the nutriment of the soul. On the one hand there were the cares of the world—these largely bother the poor and struggling; on the other hand was the deceitfulness of riches—these principally are found among the opulent and well-to-do. There was for a brief interval a struggle as to which of these should be master, but the strife soon ended in the victory of the sturdy thorns; those ruthless rivals seized for themselves all the sustenance that the soil of the heart could supply, and grew ranker and taller until the tiny corn withered and failed to grow toward perfection.

Will you not examine yourself? You think that you are

wholehearted, whereas you may be doublehearted; or, to use a simile of the prophet, baked on one side and not on the other (Hosea 7:8); or, to use the simile of a great dreamer, looking one way and rowing another. You seem to be very earnest in Christian work, but are you quite sure that your apparent devotion does not arise from a masterfulness of disposition that likes to be independent and rude? May it not be due to a fussy activity which must be engaged in many directions that the soul may escape from itself; or to a natural pity and sympathy for people which would incite you to do a similar deed even though you had never heard of Christ? Of course, you say to yourself that your motive is pure and single—that you only desire to glorify God; but in His sight it may be that you are really actuated by the natural propensities of your nature, by your desire to be first, or by your appetite for notoriety or money. The heart is so deceitful (Jer. 17:9) that it becomes us to examine ourselves with all carefulness, lest at the end of life we shall find that while we appeared to be doing God's work, we were really doing our own; and that while our friends gave us credit for great religious devotion, we were really borne along by a vain, proud, and unworthy purpose, which robbed our noblest service of all value in the sight of eternity.

As the Apostle says, the one supreme intention of every child of God should be to please God. How few of us can say with him: "Whose I am and whom I serve" (Acts 27:23); "It is a very small thing that I should be judged of you, or of man's judgment. . . . He that judgeth me is the Lord" (1 Cor. 4:3-4).

(3) LET US SEE TO IT THAT WE HAVE A PURE AND SIMPLE INTENTION. Our aim should be to set our whole soul upon one thing only—to do the will of God, so that the whole of our Christian life may be spent before the Father who sees in secret that our alms, our prayers, our fastings, should be for His eye, and His alone, and that the whole of our lives should emanate from hidden fountains where God's Spirit broods, like those fountains of the Nile hidden in the heart of the great mountains, the secret of which has defied the research of the explorer. The lamp of a holy life is the pure

intention of the soul which seeks to gain nothing for itself; which has no desire to please people or to receive their commendation; which does not shirk adversity or court the sunshine, but which sets before it as its all-sufficient goal, that God may be well-pleased, and that at the close of life's brief pilgrimage it may be said of each of us, as it was said of Enoch, who "had this testimony, that he pleased God" (Heb. 11:5).

How blessed such a life is! The light of the soul's pure intention illuminates God, duty, human love, the glory of creation, and the significance of history, literature, and art. I remember once in my life at a most important crisis, when for weeks I was torn between two strong conflicting claims, that at last I was compelled to put aside all engagements and to go alone into the midst of Nature, where I carefully examined my heart to its very depths. I found that the cause of the difficulty to ascertain God's will arose because I allowed so many personal considerations to conflict with the inner voice, and when I definitely put these aside, and stilled and quieted my life so that I became conscious of being impelled by one purpose only—to know and to do God's will—then the lamp of a pure intention shed its glow upon the path which I became assured was the chosen path for me: and since I dared from that moment to follow, all other things have been added. It was when Solomon asked that he might have a wise and understanding heart, that he might know God's purpose, that God gave him honor, wealth, and length of days (1 Kings 3:5-14). Again and again these words of Christ ring out among the deepest that He ever spoke: "Seek ye first the Kingdom of God, and His righteousness, and all these things shall be added unto you" (Matt. 6:33).

From Darkness to Light

If the lamp of the pure intention of the soul is not kept pure and clean, "How great is that darkness!" (Matt. 6:23) Our Lord alludes, of course, to the fact that when darkness settles upon the forest, the beasts steal forth, the glades resound to the roar of the lion, the cry of the jackal, the laugh of the hyena. Multitudes of beasts, that have lain quiet in their lairs while the sun was shining, now creep forth; and our Lord says that when a person's heart is set on doing God's will the lower and baser passions of his nature—like so many beasts of prey—remain in their hiding places. But as soon as the blur comes and the soul ceases to live for the one intense purpose of pleasing God, then darkness steals upon the house of life, and all manner of evil and unclean things, that otherwise would be shamed into silence and secrecy, begin to reveal themselves. "How great is that darkness!" (Matt. 6:23) If I am addressing people who are conscious that there is a darkness upon life, upon truth, upon the Word of God; if they are perplexed and plagued by the intrusion of evil things which fill them with misgiving—let me urge them to ask God to cleanse the thoughts of their hearts by the inspiration of His Holy Spirit, that they may perfectly love Him, and worthily magnify His Holy Name.

CHAPTER SEVENTEEN

THE LESSON
OF BIRDS AND FLOWERS

(Matt. 6:25-34)

Thee Eye—that is, the pure
Intention—of the soul ceases to be single when it is diverted by the covetous desire to hoard up money. It may also
be diverted by the constant pressure of anxiety. So as our
Lord has been dealing with avarice, which is the special
temptation of the well-to-do and prosperous, so now He
turns to deal with the special temptation of the poor, which
is anxious care.

Of course, wealth has its anxieties as well as poverty. A
rich man, whose wealth may be swept away in an hour by
a panic on the Stock Exchange, may toss all night long on a
sleepless pillow, while a laboring man, who cannot see beyond the needs of the week, may be sleeping soundly
through the small hours. But the anxiety of those who, in
any event, will always be certain of being provided with the
necessaries of life is surely less excusable than the care of
the poor man, who has no nest egg against a rainy day. He
may at any moment fall sick or lose his job, and may be
condemned to see first his home, and then his scanty wardrobe, stripped first of little comforts, and then of necessaries, and, when nearly everything is gone, his wife and
children becoming every day paler, thinner, and hungrier.

Our Lord and Poverty

It is to be noticed that our Lord's tone is much gentler and more tender as He turns to address the poor who toil for their daily bread, and whose slenderly provided table is often shadowed with the specter of anxiety about tomorrow's provision. In the former paragraph (Matt. 6:19-23) there was a tone of stern remonstrance as our Lord spoke of the absurdity of setting the heart on things which the thief might steal and the moth corrupt; but here there is a touch of tender pity and sympathy as He says, three times over, "Don't be anxious" (or "Take no thought," Matt. 6:25, 31, 34). He never forgot that He was a Child of the laboring class; that His mother, at His birth, had brought the gift of the poor to the Temple; and that from boyhood He had been accustomed to poverty. His frequent speech about patching garments and using old bottleskins, about the price of sparrows, and the scanty pittance of a laborer's life, indicate that His mind was habituated to the experiences of the poor. Ever since He had left His mother's home, abandoning the trade which had secured slender provision for Himself and others, He had known what it was to have no shelter for the night, and to subsist on the chance gifts of charity and friendship.

Foresight vs. Foreboding

The words "take no thought" of the *King James Version* do not represent the true force of the phrase used by our Lord. We are endowed with the faculty of foresight, of scanning the horizon, of anticipating the dark, low storm clouds, and of taking in our sails. He that "provideth not for his own," says the Apostle, "is worse than an unbeliever" (1 Tim. 5:8, ASV)—and such provision involves foresight. But there is all the difference in the world between foresight and foreboding. It is the latter, not the former, that our Lord speaks out against. A wise person must lay his carefully considered plans, and work for their accomplishment. The farmer must sow in the autumn for the coming harvest. The importer must arrange, months beforehand, for the arrival of foreign produce at a given time when the home markets will be ripe for it. The manufacturer is already preparing the season's goods for next year. But when all has been done that can be done, our Lord says: "You must leave the results with God: you have done all that you could do; now leave the results with your heavenly Father."

The words used by the *American Standard Version*, instead of "Take no thought," are "Be not anxious" (Matt. 6:25, 31, 34). The Greek word implies that a person's mind may be divided and broken up from the main object and purpose of existence by the constant pressure of foreboding care. As the force of a stream is lessened if the waters are diverted into two or three channels, so the force of a person's heart and life dwindle when the perpetual dread of failure and loss call off his soul from its primary intention and aim. How can one do his best work if he is paralyzed by foreboding as to the contents of tomorrow? When the mind is stricken with panic, tossed to and fro with distraction, and filled with pictures of penury and destitution; when every sight of wife and family only awakens deeper dread of what may await them; when paragraphs in the daily paper prophesy the pressure of hard times—how can a soul do its best work? It is divided, distracted, and torn.

Food and Raiment, Truth and Love

In this paragraph our Lord is dealing principally with food and raiment—the simple needs of an agricultural and pastoral people. And there are myriads around us on whose lips these questions are perpetual. "What shall we eat? . . . What shall we drink?" Wherewithal shall we be clothed?" (Matt. 6:31) Clearly we are creatures of two worlds. Our minds hunger for truth and our hearts for love. "Man shall not live by bread alone" (Matt. 4:4). And there are anxieties for others, for their clothing in the garments of purity and holiness, for their feeding on the fare of the truth of God, and for their housing in the love of God, which are far more pressing and imperative than the care for their physical and temporal well-being. All these dividing thoughts are equally forbidden when our Lord says, "Do not be anxious."

Anxiousness about Food

Three times over we hear this sweet refrain, *Be not anxious. . . . Be not therefore anxious. . . . Be not therefore anxious* (Matt. 6.25, 31, 34, ASV).

Do not be anxious about food, whether of the body, the mind, or the heart.

(1) *The life [is] more than the food* (Matt. 6:25). When God gave life He caused it to be dependent on the sustenance which is provided from field and orchard. It is by His own contrivance and ordering that we must be nourished by the fruits of the soil; and surely He is not so unreasonable as to create the need and to contrive the perpetual recurrence of appetite, and then fail in meeting both. If He has given life, does not that gift implicate its support? He must have had a purpose in the donation of life to every one of us, and surely He will be responsible for the food which is necessary, if His original purpose is not to be frustrated!

(2) *Are ye not of much more value than the birds of the heaven?* (Matt. 6:26)

As our Lord was speaking, flocks of pigeons were flying overhead; swallows were darting in the air for insects; sparrows were flying, chirping, from stone to stone in search of food. All this wonderful and multitudinous bird-life, so blithe and happy, was a matter of constant interest to the child-heart of Jesus, and seemed to rebuke foreboding fear. These little feathered creatures do not perform a stroke of work to produce their food, but only take what the Creator gives, as He opens His hand to supply their need. That which He gives them they gather. You may walk for days through the forests and find no dead bird. I grant you that the wild things of the woods do perish at certain seasons, but before we charge this on any want of care on the part of the Creator it would have to be shown that the balance of Creation had not been disturbed by human interference. Do we not prognosticate the advent of a hard winter by the abundance of berries on the hedges, and is not that the Divine provision for the birds of the air, who have neither storehouse nor barn? Surely if our Heavenly Father feeds these tiny creatures, which are the pensioners on His bounty, who can do nothing to help themselves, He will not be unmindful of His children! "Your heavenly Father feedeth them—are ye not much better than they?"

(3) Besides, *Which of you by being anxious can add one cubit unto the measure of his life?* (6:27, ASV) or (as the margin suggests) to *his stature.* Clearly the Lord is not speaking of our physical stature, for it would be an unheard-of-thing, and one for which none would be specially solicitous, to add a foot and a half to his stature! He is evidently alluding to the length of human life, of which the Psalmist David says: "Thou hast made my days as an handbreadth" (Ps. 39:5). After all, the length of our years has been fixed by God; and we are immortal till our work is done. All our anxiety will not add an inch or a yard to the path that we are destined to tread between our cradle and our grave. God has measured it out with exact precision, and He will supply all our need until the day's march is ended and the day's labor fulfilled.

Anxiousness about Clothing

Do not be anxious about clothing.

(1) *All the animals have their covering,* the lamb its wool, the kitten its fur, the fledgling its fluffy down—but humans are born naked, and require clothing for modesty and warmth. This was evidently the intention of the Creator, and He has filled the world with the materials of our supply. May we not hold Him responsible to meet the needs of His own Creation? Did He not clothe Adam and Eve with the skins of beasts already slain in sacrifice? Does He not provide for the soul the white and dazzling raiment of imputed righteousness with which we are arrayed before all worlds? And will He neglect the body? "The body" is more "than raiment" (Matt. 6:25). If He bestows the one so wondrously wrought, surely He will give the other.

(2) Besides, look again into *nature at the growth of the flowers.* At the time when Jesus spoke the fields were carpeted with wild flowers. Palestine in those days was the land, not of milk only, bespeaking the rich pastures, but also of honey, because the air was redolent with the breath of myriads of wild flowers, bespangling the pastures, clustering in the hedgerows, and hiding in the woodland glades. Theirs was

140

as careless a life as that of the birds. "They toil not, neither do they spin." For some, no doubt—the exotics of our greenhouses and nurseries—there must be excessive care in the provision of greenhouse heat and the experienced skill of the horticulturist. The Lord was not alluding to these, but to the flowers in the grass, which grew amid the wilds of nature and in the gardens of the poor, and were cut down by the scythe or gathered to perish quickly in the hot hand of a careless child. To Him these were exquisitely beautiful. Of the Son of Man it may be said with peculiar appropriateness that the humblest flower that blew awakened thoughts too deep for tears. The wild flowers of His native land were, in His eyes, attired in garments more rare and beautiful than the gorgeous magnificence of Israel's greatest king. "Solomon in all his glory was not arrayed like one of these" (Matt. 6:29). How quietly they grew, far from the clatter of machinery, the throw of the shuttle, the revolution of the wheel! How modestly and unobtrusively they concealed themselves from the glare of publicity in dells and woodland glades! How simple in their chaste and lovely garb!

What do they teach? Was not this the lesson of their growth that God loves the beautiful, and expends thought and skill in the flowers' production? He might have made the world without a daisy, and human life without childhood. Considerations of stern utility might have imposed their rigorous law on the creation of all things visible and invisible; but since the Creator clothes with beauty the short-lived flowers of the wilds, the ephemeral insects of a summer day, the shells of the minute creatures that build up the solid fabric of the rocks by the countless myriads of their tiny homes, surely this prodigality, this lavishness, this prolific superabundance of creativeness, must mean that He can and will withhold no good thing from them that fear Him (Ps. 84:11), least of all clothes to cover their nakedness and give them warmth.

Of course we must fulfill our part. We are not to imitate the careless improvident life of the lower orders of Creation. We must certainly sow and reap and gather into barns; we must certainly toil and spin; but when we have

141

done all, we must fall back on the Divine Providence, believing that it is vain for us to rise up early, and sit up late, and eat the bread of sorrows, because our God will give us all we need, even while we sleep. He will not allow His children to starve or go unsheltered, unclothed and unshod. "Therefore take no thought saying, What shall we eat, or what shall we drink, or wherewithal shall we be clothed?" (Matt. 6:31)

Anxiousness Is Heathenism

Be not anxious: It is heathenism. "After all these things do the Gentiles seek" (Matt. 6:32). The blue waters of the Mediterranean were almost within sight, reminding the Speaker of the great nations that lay on their shores, and launched their navies on her bosom. He knew that while some might be feeling after God, if haply they might find Him, or be found of Him (Acts 17:27), the bulk of them had refused to retain Him in their knowledge, and had exchanged the Creator for the creature (Rom. 1:21-25). He knew, moreover, that to most of them there was either no God or else they deemed Him too far removed from earthly things to have any interest in their lives. Of what good, then, was it to pray to Him? For many the supreme conception was that fate, destiny, or chance was the presiding arbiter and ruler of their existence.

Amid the darkness of such conceptions, what could be expected but that the grim specter of care should haunt every life, and sit uninvited at every table? When one has no knowledge of the Divine Fatherhood, what defenses has he against sudden, wild alarms, or insidious, corroding care?

But those whom our Lord addressed had been taught to regard God as their Heavenly Father; and to us the revelation is more explicit than even to them. We know that we are children of God, begotten unto a living hope, partakers of the Divine Nature, adopted into the Divine family. We are conscious that the Spirit of Sonship is in our hearts, witnessing that we have been born from above. We realize that we are not only sons and daughters; but heirs—heirs of God and joint heirs with Christ. Our Father loves us, knows our frame, views us with paternal pitifulness, and longs to bring us to glory. He has given us His Son and His Spirit. Surely He will not withhold the food and raiment needed for our bodies. He has given the infinitely great; surely He will not grudge the small. "He that spared not His own Son, but delivered Him up for us all, how shall He not with Him also freely give us all things?" (Rom. 8:32)

Anxiousness for the Kingdom of God

Be not anxious: There are other and greater interests at stake. "Seek ye first the Kingdom of God and His righteousness" (Matt. 6:33). It is the great object of God that His long-expected Kingdom should come; that purity as of the dawn should replace the reign of corruption and night; and that life should replace death, and love hatred. For this He has been at work all through the long centuries. He will not stay His hand till angel voices proclaim that the kingdoms of this world have become the kingdoms of His Christ.

In His great kindness He has called us in to help Him accomplish His great purpose, and lays it upon us as a special burden that we should not rest, nor allow Him to rest, until the Kingdom come, and His will be done on earth as in Heaven. For this we must labor and pray. Be anxious for this, if you will. Lie awake at night to mourn over the condition of lost souls, if you can. Expend tears and prayers in untiring supplication for the lost. As you care for God's concerns, God will care for yours.

The great contractor who has undertaken a line of a railway, or the construction of a vast reservoir among the hills, knows the necessity of providing for the well-being of the thousands of workers engaged with their spades or trowels. If they are to do work which will not disgrace him, he at least must see that their physical health and well-being are guaranteed. Is it likely, then, that God will be less careful and thoughtful of his own children, whom He has called into fellowship with Himself? Does He not know that we do our best work when we are free from anxious care? Is He so unrighteous as to forget us, who labor day and night for the purpose which lies so near His heart? It is impossible to suppose it; but as we seek His Kingdom, He will seek our welfare with both hands, earnestly and carefully. Rest on this promise, which He who is incarnate truth gave: "All these things shall be added" (Matt. 6:33).

Anxiousness Can Rob Strength

Be not anxious, as it will not rob tomorrow of its anxiety, but it will deprive today of its strength. "Take, therefore, no thought for the morrow, for the morrow [will be anxious for itself, ASV]. Sufficient unto the day is the evil thereof" (Matt. 6:34). From these words it is clear that every morrow will have some anxiety, and every day some evil. No sky without some clouds to fleck its blue, no lot without its crook, no Paschal lamb without its bitter herbs. We shall never be totally free from anxiety of one kind or another until we have passed the gates of pearl.

However much we worry today in the hope of anticipating and cancelling the worry of tomorrow, we shall not succeed. There always will be something to cause us annoyance, perplexity, and chagrin. But as the day, so will the strength be (Deut. 33:25)—just enough, with not one grain to spare. Indeed, the anxiety will be permitted to drive us to the strong for strength, as a hard winter will drive even a timid deer down to the homes of men.

To worry, therefore, about tomorrow is to overpress the strength of today, which is enough for today's burden, but not enough for today's and tomorrow's also. If you try to carry today's burdens by actual endurance, and tomorrow's by anticipation, what wonder that you break down, aging prematurely, and sowing plentiful silver among your young black locks.

For all these reasons let us not be anxious. "Be careful for nothing, but in everything by prayer and supplication, with thanksgiving, let your requests be made known unto God, and the peace of God, which passeth all understanding, shall keep your hearts and minds, through Christ Jesus" (Phil. 4:6-7).

CHAPTER EIGHTEEN

TO THEM
THAT ARE WITHOUT

(Matt. 7:1-6)

As long as we are in this mortal life we shall necessarily come into contact with those whose lives are godless and evil. Evil people and seducers will wax worse and worse. People will always abound who will not consent to wholesome words, even the words of our Lord Jesus Christ, and the doctrine which is according to godliness. There will always be perverse disputings of people of corrupt minds, destitute of the truth, and enemies to whatever is pure, lovely, holy, and of good report. In this paragraph of the Sermon on the Mount our Lord sets Himself to show us how to act toward such people. It is clear that the Master had no desire that His servants should retire from human society, but should live among people as salt and light, arresting the progress of corruption, and abashing the evil deeds that hide under the cover of darkness; but, in addition to the quiet influence of our character, there will always be scope for a further exercise of Christian principle. In what direction, and to what extent, is this to take effect, and by what laws is it to be governed? In answer to these questions our Lord lays down a general principle, which is removed as far as possible from that which is popular in the world. He says: Whatever you do, think, or say about others must be in precise accordance with what you would like them to do, think, or say about yourself. "Judge not . . . for with what judgment ye judge, ye shall be judged. And with what measure ye mete, it shall be measured to you again" (Matt. 7:1-2). All things whatever you want people to do to you, do you to them; and all things whatever you would *not* have them do to you, do not do so to them.

It is clear that there are in this paragraph three circles of people with whom we are constantly thrown into contact. First, our *Associates and Neighbors*, whose characters and conduct constantly pass in review before us; secondly, *the Erring Ones*, whose motes trouble us; and, thirdly, *the Dogs and Swine*, the notoriously vicious and profane.

Our Associates and Neighbors

As to our Associates and Neighbors, our Lord says:

(1) *"Judge not"* (Matt. 7:1). We need hardly say that there is a sense in which we are bound to form careful judgments on those around us. The judgment is one of the noblest faculties of our moral life, and our surest safeguard from the sharks that infest the seas. The young girl must use it of the man who is seeking to engage her affections; the young man must use it of another man who offers him a partnership; the seeker after truth must use it of the teacher who professes to be able to lead him. There is no prayer that we need to make more often or more fervently than that God would give us right judgment in all things. "He that is spiritual judgeth all things" (1 Cor. 2:15).

But the judgment prohibited by our Lord is altogether different from this, and is that spirit of censoriousness and unkindness which is always lying in wait for others, and making strong and uncharitable statements on the most superficial view of their words and actions, without trying to understand the motives by which they have been actuated or the difficulties of their positions.

The natural man is proud, haughty, and self-opinionated. He has a great contempt of and a great prejudice toward those who do not belong to his own sect or party. He is, therefore, very censorious of them, making faults where there are none, and aggravating them where they are.

146

When he has formed, however hastily, his judgment, he is not content with contemplating it for himself, but takes every opportunity of venting it in word and act. When such people win another to their party, they are perfectly willing to condone his faults. If not, they will not scruple to extinguish him and his influence by poisoning the minds of his neighbors and contemporaries. This sin of censorious judgment is a constant peril to us all, and one against which we need to watch and pray.

Beware lest you have a secret joy in seeing that another who had borne an irreproachable character has failed! Beware lest you form your estimate of another on idle stories, suspicions, suggestions, and surmises, and without sufficient evidence! Beware of seeking after a reputation for quickness in estimating the true worth of others, since the desire to maintain such a reputation is fraught with temptation! Beware of speaking of the faults of others, unless you have prayed about them first! Beware of uttering your criticisms unless there is some end to be gained in warning others! Beware of speaking of others till you have looked at home! Remember the proverb about glass houses!

Some people seem unable to form a generous estimate of any. According to them there is always some evil motive behind apparent goodness, which detracts from all merit or virtue. "Yes, he does seem religious and humane, but there is a rich old relative in the background, and it is all-important to keep on impressing him." Or, "Yes, he is religious enough just now, but there is a lady in question, and he is perfectly right in the way he is taking to win her." It is a sad and miserable state of mind to have no eyes but for wounds, bruises, and putrefying sores, and to find these beneath the surface when they do not appear to the eyes of others. Many young men and women among us can hardly indulge in any language but that of depreciation.

(2) *Our ignorance of most of the facts should give us pause before passing harsh and censorious judgments.* Take this, for instance: A merchant was thought to be very selfish with his money. He was known to be very rich, and yet when asked for donations he gave always a small sum ($20) where his neighbors thought he ought to give $100. He was

therefore in ill odor for miserliness and greed. This went on for years, and many closed their hearts against him. One of his friends, however, who felt that there might be some other explanation, set himself to ascertain the facts. It was with some difficulty that he finally discovered that this much-abused man was supporting a large family of poor relatives. He educated them well, and put them out in life with no stingy hand. They lived in another town, and no one knew of the source of their income. Their benefactor never allowed his left hand to know what his right hand did. Here was a man whom all were misjudging because they did not know all the facts. Is it a solitary instance?

(3) *The fact that we cannot judge others adversely without revealing ourselves may also make us pause.* Someone who imputes low motives to the conduct of another is probably conscious of their presence within himself. He is already actuated by them, or would be if he were in the place of the person he criticizes. He has no higher standard for another than that which rules in his own breast, and almost unconsciously in his criticisms he is revealing his own soul.

(4) *It is inevitable that our harsh judgments of others will come back on ourselves.* A man receives back what he gives. There is an automatic law of compensation in society. Kindness begets kindness, censoriousness begets censoriousness. Ishmael's hands were against everyone, and every man's hand was against him. Adonibezek cut off the thumbs and great toes of seventy kings; and as it was done by him it was done to him (Jud. 1:5-7). Haman was hanged on the gallows which he had erected for Mordecai (Es. 7:10). Many Jews, who banned all others as heathen dogs, are themselves banned. The world may fitly be compared to a vast field in which each person drops his seed, and it comes back to him, not just the same that it was when he dropped it in, any more than in the autumn you reap from the earth the blackberry which you hid in its broad bosom in the spring, but something which truly corresponds to it. Every gift has its return, every act its rebound, every voice its echo. The Lord states the alternative in another similar discourse, when He says: "Give, and it shall be given unto you; good measure, pressed down, and shaken together,

and running over, shall men give into your bosom. For with the same measure that ye mete withal it shall be measured to you again" (Luke 6:38).

"Wherefore judge nothing before the time, until the Lord come, who will both bring to light the hidden things of darkness, and make manifest the counsels of the hearts, and then shall each man have his praise from God" (1 Cor. 4:5, ASV). Especially guard against *prejudice*—that is, prejudgment. Remember the dogs and swine in the makeup of your own heart, and you must see to it that their presence does not trample what is purest, noblest, and best, and hurt men and women who, if you knew and understood them more fully, would attract your loving veneration. Remember the words with which our Lord prefaced His warning against censorious judgment: "Be ye therefore merciful, as your Father also is merciful" (Luke 6:36).

The Erring Ones

As to the Erring:

(1) *Consider the beam that is in your own eye* (Matt. 7:3). The beam is, of course, a log, rafter, or joist, and is the extreme contrast with a tiny chip or splint of wood which is light enough to float in the air. A child can understand what our Lord means when He employs a well-known Jewish proverb to give a simple flavor to His speech.

(2) *By nature we are extremely prone to put other people right.* We behold the mote that is in our brother's eye till we can think of nothing else. All the good qualities he possesses weigh lighter than swans' down against that one inconsistency that presents itself to us at each mention of his name. Finally, we go to him with the fixed resolve of ridding him of his mote, saying, "Let me pull out the mote that is in your eye." Now in all this there would be nothing to condemn—indeed, there would be much to commend—if it were done lovingly, humbly, and after the due confession and putting away from our own life of all inconsistency and sin; but it is the height of absurdity to attempt to extract the mote when your own vision is distorted by the presence of your unextracted beam. How dare you presume to deal with the faultiness of others when your own faults have not

been corrected! It is like Satan rebuking sin. Well may people cry, "Physician, heal thyself" (Luke 4:23).

(3) *It is evidently a very delicate operation to correct the faults of others.* Our Lord compares it to the extraction of a little piece of grit, or dust, or a minute insect, from an inflamed eye. A clumsy hand may well make the matter worse. Only the tenderest hand can be trusted for the operation; and, if I might choose, let me have one who has himself suffered, being tempted. It is only He, who has been tempted in all points like as we are, though without sin, who can be trusted to deal with our inner temptations, inconsistencies, and failures (Heb. 4:15). It is a person whose own transgressions have been forgiven according to the multitude of God's tender mercies who can teach transgressors His ways.

(4) *First cast out the beam out of thine own eye* (Matt. 7:5). There is a beam there, if you only knew it. We look at our neighbor's errors with a microscope, but at our own through the wrong end of a telescope. We have two sets of weights and measures—one for home use and the other for foreign. Every vice has two names; and we call it by the flattering and minimizing one when we commit it, and by the ugly one when our neighbor does it. Everybody can see the hump on his friend's shoulders, but it takes some effort to see our own. A blind guide is bad enough, but a blind oculist is still more ridiculous. The more we know ourselves the more pity we shall show others; the less likely to form rash and harsh judgments; the more sweet and tender we shall be in trying to make people better.

(5) *Then thou shalt see clearly* (Matt. 7:5). Only the pure heart sees; and when once some heart-sin is put away a flood of light pours on all things in heaven and on earth. We see sin as we never saw it, and the love of God and the grace of our Lord Jesus Christ.

> Heaven above is softer blue,
>   Earth around is sweeter green;
> Something shines in every hue
>   Christless eyes have never seen.
> Birds with gladder songs o'erflow,

Flowers with brighter beauties shine,
While Christ whispers in my ear,
I am His and He is mine.

The Dogs and Swine

As to Dogs and Swine—Use a wise discrimination (Matt. 7:6).
Suppose a priest, on coming out of the Temple, encounters
a hungry dog—one of those yelping, voracious, unclean
animals, which are the scavengers and pests of Oriental
cities—would it be seemly for him to return to the Temple
and take a piece of the flesh which was reserved from the
sacrifices for the use of priests, and therefore *holy*, and give
it to the dog for food? He might relieve the creature's hunger, but not with such food as that.

Or suppose a man, carrying a bag of pearls through a
forest, were to encounter a hog, would it be wise or seemly
for him to place the pearls before it, when it needed acorns?
Similarly, it is unseemly to offer the sacraments of our holy
religion or the forgiveness of Christ's Gospel to the notoriously unclean and untrue, or to discuss the sacred mysteries of the Epistle to the Ephesians with those who are set
on coarse and carnal pleasures. First, their natures must be
changed. They must be born from above. Old things must
pass away, and all things become new. Then, when their
hearts of stone have been removed and hearts of flesh substituted, their souls will hunger after the Divine mysteries,
and will be able to appreciate them in such a way as to
justify us in presenting them. The raven may feed on carri-
on, but the dove will return to Noah's Ark until she can
find her natural food. (Gen. 8:7-12).

The Blood and the Spirit

For all this we need something which was not fully revealed when our Lord was speaking, but has been revealed
since. The soul which stands before this high ideal is filled
with despair until it remembers—first, that the precious
Blood cleanses from all sin and shortcoming; and, secondly,
at the Holy Spirit longs to make possible and real these
heavenly ideals. May that Blood cleanse and that Spirit renew and perfect you and me!

CHAPTER NINETEEN

THE ROYALTY
OF OUR LIFE

(Matt. 7:7-12)

Ⅰt is inevitable, as the Lord has clearly implied in the preceding words, that, so long as we are in the world, we must come in contact with its evil. There will be inconsistencies that we shall be tempted to judge, motes and beams that we shall have to extract, and swine or dogs with whom we must reckon. It cannot be child's play for any of us. And if we are to keep ourselves unspotted from the world, and unsubdued by the inward power of sin, we must have resort to the weapon of All-Prayer. Therefore, our Lord turns from the exhortations of the preceding paragraph (Matt. 7:1-6) to these injunctions concerning prayer. It was as though He said: "You will never succeed in being or doing what I say unless your lives are full of persistent and prevailing prayer."

It may be that there is an even wider range of thought. As we review this matchless conception of a holy life, so far removed above anything the human mind has conceived; as we recall the Beatitudes of the opening sentences, the searching fulfillment of the older Law, the warnings against an impaired intention of the soul, against ostentation, covetousness, and care—our hearts might well faint at the immensity of the task before us. And as we think of His demand—that we should be perfect as our Heavenly Father is perfect, that we should be filled with a Divine love, and that we should always treat others as we wish they should treat us—we might again cry, "Who is sufficient for these things?" (2 Cor. 2:16) To answer this double attitude, which is indeed one, the Lord says: *"Pray!* What is impossible with man is possible with God. Pray!"

We have here two words which prove that the entire paragraph is closely joined together—"If ye *then* being evil. . . . *Therefore*, all things whatsoever" (Matt. 7:11-12). The exhortation to prayer is followed by an analogy, then by an injunction.

Exhortation to Prayer

(1) *"Ask"* (Matt. 7:7). Our Master knew well how much it would mean to us that His own lips should utter that word, but He did not hesitate to speak it. As Son of God, He knew all that asking would do for us; and, as Son of Man, He had often proved the value of the practice He inculcated. *Ask*, He said. It was as though He loved to dwell on the word. See! He repeats it, not once or twice, but four times over. "Everyone that *asketh* receiveth. . . . "if his son *ask* bread. . . . if he *ask* a fish. . . . good things to them that *ask"* (Matt. 7:8-11). It seems as though our Lord would do away with the formality and stateliness that attach to too many of our prayers, and teach us that praying is just asking, and asking as a child would ask. Adults shrink from asking for a favor from other adults, but a little child has no reserve with its father. In the simplest and most artless manner it asks for what it wants, and with no doubt at all that the father will gladly hasten to respond. "Thus," says our Lord, "ask God for what you want, as long ago you asked your parents; and do it without self-consciousness."

"Everyone that asketh receiveth" (Matt. 7:8). Emerson tells us that he preached his first sermon from these words, having obtained his divisions from the blunt saying of a field laborer, who said that men are always praying, and always being heard. His divisions, therefore, were: (1) Men are always praying; (2) all their prayers are granted; (3) we must beware, then, what we ask. The second point is the doubtful one. Is it true that all our prayers are granted? Not surely in the way that we ask, as we shall see; but in some way. No prayer that we utter which is based on a real need—nothing that we sincerely ask for which is not answered somehow, somewhen, somewhere.

With too many of us, alas! there is a failure in the art of receptiveness. We ask, but we fail to take. We send out our letter in the outgoing mail, but never ask if there is a reply addressed to us. We send an ocean cablegram asking for a consignment of heavenly treasure, but never go down to the wharf to ascertain if it has arrived, and to claim it.

(2) *Seek* (Matt. 7:7). You ask for a gift; you seek for something you have lost, or for some valuable treasure. The miner gropes along the corridors of the mine for his quest; the pearl fisher dives in search of goodly pearls; the woman who had lost her silver piece lit a candle, and swept and searched her house diligently till she found it. Seek, says our Lord. If you have lost your peace with God, the blessed consciousness of His presence, power in service, or any other spiritual gift, do not settle down content to live without it, but seek diligently until you find it. "Your heart shall live that seek God" (Ps. 69:32). If you have heard of some gift or grace which others possess, and may be equally yours as theirs, seek it. Seek it as people seek for hidden treasure or for goodly pearls, or as the philosophers were wont to seek for the substance which should turn everything into gold, as explorers seek for the secret of the North Pole, or as scientists search for the secrets which Nature holds back from all but reverent and persevering inquiry. "Seek Him that maketh the seven stars and Orion, and turneth the shadow of death into the morning" (Amos 5:8).

"He that seeketh, findeth" (Matt. 7:8). "If thou criest after knowledge, and liftest up thy voice for understanding; if thou seekest her as silver, and searchest for her as for hid treasures, then shalt thou understand the fear of the Lord, and find the knowledge of God" (Prov. 2:3-5). We may not always find just what we seek, but we may come on something much better, and more satisfying. Abram and the patriarchs sought a country, but they all died in tents, the shifting memorials of their pilgrimage. The philosophers of the Middle Ages did not find the golden stone, but they laid the foundations of modern chemistry. You may not ever obtain that special opportunity of blessing others which you have long desired; but in your willingness to take a subordinate position, in your meekness and humility, you will certainly win a moral and spiritual influence that is incomparably greater. The resolute seeker finds. He starts out to raise crops of golden grain from the brown fields, and as he patiently drives his plow, a metallic chink of the share on metal reveals that he has discovered a treasure trove.

(3) *Knock* (Matt. 7:7). We ask for a gift; we seek something we have lost; but we knock for admittance to the house of our friend. A door stands between us and the master of the house, which can only be opened from within. Then we knock; at first quietly, and then more vehemently and loudly, till we hear the drawing back of bolt and bar, and see the door open. We need the gifts of God, and are thankful for the treasures which follow earnest, prayerful search; but we should desire, above all, to enjoy face-to-face friendship with Himself. Sometimes the door of fellowship stands wide open, and we can enter without hindrance. At other times it seems as though God has hidden His face and withdrawn Himself. Those are the times when we must knock. How often it has been the experience of the saints that, as they have stood waiting and knocking, the door has been opened as by an invisible hand, and the times of greatest difficulty at the beginning have been those of greatest liberty at the close!

"To him that knocketh it shall be opened" (Matt. 7:8). There is no doubt or hesitation in our Lord's assurance. In another paragraph He speaks of those who shall stand outside and knock, pleading, "Lord, Lord, open unto us," and He shall say, "Depart" (Luke 13:25-27); but that dread parable has nothing to do with access into the presence and the fellowship of God, of which the Master is here treating. Persistency, and urgency, which will not be denied, are both dear to the heart of God, and are certain to win from Him a loving and favorable response. "Though [the vision] tarry, wait for it: because it will surely come, it will not tarry" (Hab. 2:3).

Bread and Fish, Stones and Serpents

Bread and fish were the simple fare of the Galilean peasants whom our Lord addressed on the shores of their own beautiful lake—the bread as the necessary staff of life; the fish as an appetizing addition. Little children, in their simplicity, might sometimes mistake a stone for one of the small loaves of the Oriental shape and fashion, or a serpent for a fish. But, even though the heart of a human father is fallen and evil, it cannot be supposed for an instant that he would give the child what it asked. His love would at once withhold his hand. He would say: "No, little one, the stone is not food, and the serpent would sting and poison you. I cannot give it to you. But see, here is what you want— bread and fish." So it often happens that in this mortal life of ours, where the shadows fall so dense and dark, and we are obliged to grope in the twilight, we are hungry with immeasurable appetite, and think that only this or the other boon will satisfy our souls. We clamor for a stone, thinking it to be bread, or cry out for the glittering serpent, supposing it to be a dainty that will titillate our palate. But as the earthly father refused, notwithstanding his weakness and evil, much more will God refuse. "No," He says; "My child, I cannot, for love's sake, give it to you; but, see, here is bread indeed, and here the fish—eat, drink, and be satisfied."

Again, God sometimes gives things that appear to be stones and serpents, but they turn out to be bread and fish. The mother of St. Augustine prayed to God that He would not let her beloved son go to Rome, because she dreaded the persecutions which were threatening the city. He went, notwithstanding, and it was in Italy that he found Christ. Referring to this incident in his life in after years, he says: "What was it, O my God, that she sought of Thee with many tears? Was it not that Thou wouldest not let me set sail for Rome? But Thou, in Thy deep counsels, and listening to the hinge of her desire, didst disregard the thing which she asked for, that Thou mightest do in me that which she was ever asking—the conversion of my soul."

Do not be surprised if there are placed on your table tasty dishes that threaten to break your teeth and disagree with your digestion. Since God has put them there—and He is good—you will find them in the highest degree nutritious. Though they be the reverse of the Prophet's vision—bitter to the mouth (Rev. 10:9-10)—they will prove to be wholesome, and sweet to the digestion.

Or take a third case. Suppose a hungry child asks for bread and fish. Its father, though evil, will not give it something which would defy its powers of digestion. Even if the father suffered the extremities of starvation, he would endure them rather than respond thus to his child's artless faith. We, therefore, may go with large requests to our God, asking for what we need, in the certain faith that He will only give us good things. He will substitute the blessing we would crave if we knew as much as He does of the heart of people. What a comfort it is to know that God gives only good things. What He withholds is good; what He gives is good; what He substitutes in His answer to our petitions is good—nay, good is not strong enough. He gives always the best.

It should be remembered that our God gives not only the necessaries, but also some luxuries and comforts of life. The Lord prepared for His hungry friends, exhausted by the labors of the night, not bread alone, but fish. "When they got out upon the land they see a fire of coals there, and fish laid thereon, and bread" (John 21:9, ASV). It was as though in that last breakfast with Him the Master desired to teach that in all coming time He would give His faithful disciples the daily supply of their recurring wants, together with the warmth of human love, which ministers to the sense of enjoyment as well as to present need.

This is a great consolation in prayer. We can ask for anything and everything we want; we may be sure that no good thing will be withholden from those who walk uprightly (Ps. 84:11); but we may also be sure that God loves us too well to give anything that would hurt us.

Probably our lives are meager and impoverished when they might become full of good things, because we fail to ask. Notice our Lord's words: "How much more shall your Father which is in heaven give good things to them that ask Him" (Matt. 7:11). Is not the Apostle James right when He says, "Ye have not because ye ask not? "That is the one reason. Or, "Because ye ask amiss, that ye may consume it upon your lusts" (James 4:2-3). That is the second reason. Either not to pray, or to pray from selfish motives, shuts us out of much Divine helpfulness which otherwise would be ours. Our Lord puts into our hands the key to the vaults in God's bank. It is our fault if grace does not abound in us, and if we are poor when we might be rich.

That Golden Rule

"Therefore, all things whatsoever ye would that men should do to you, do ye even so to them" (Matt. 7:12). With much reason this has been called the Golden Rule.

Gibbon reminds us that in a negative form it was in vogue four centuries before the Christian Era. But this is not to be wondered at, since Christ was in the world from the first. "There was the true Light, even the Light which lighteth every man coming into the world. He was in the world, and the world was made through Him, and the world knew Him not" (John 1:9-10).

But for the positive form of this truth, and for the power by which it can operate in our selfish, evil hearts, we are entirely indebted to Jesus Christ's teaching and inspiration.

Put into common English, this precept may be rendered: Put yourself in another's place; treat him as you would wish to be treated under similar circumstances; do not deal with him as you would not wish to be dealt with. The Lord, in effect, goes back to the words which stand at the beginning of the chapter, saying, "Judge as you would like to be judged; measure as you would like it to be measured to you" (Matt. 7:1-2, author's paraphrase).

The principle, of course, as He says, is witnessed "by the Law and the Prophets" (Matt. 7:12). We find it stated in the second great commandment: "Thou shalt love thy neighbor as thyself" (Lev. 19:18; Matt. 22:39). It is *fundamental*, underpinning the whole structure of human society. It is *equitable*, because all people are more nearly equal than might be inferred from considering their outward circumstances. It is *portable*, like a tape measure an artisan carries in his pocket for measuring any work he may be called to estimate.

The Emperor Severus was so charmed by the excellence of this rule that he ordered it to be inscribed on the most notable parts of the palace, and on many of the public buildings. But though the maxim has attracted so much attention and admiration, it is powerless to effect any great reform apart from the Holy Spirit. Therefore it is that in the other version of this paragraph (Luke 11:13), our Lord asks, "How much more shall your heavenly Father give the Holy Spirit to them that ask Him?" After all, it is only they who have stood under the open sky of Pentecost, who have received their share of that blessed enduement and infilling, which is the right of every believer, but which is too seldom claimed, who can go through the world practicing always the Golden Rule of love. It is only they who by the Holy Spirit have been brought into living union with Christ, who receive hour by hour the full current of His life, who can go on loving people with the prodigality of affection, tempered, of course, with wisdom and discretion such as avail to fill up to the brim the full measure of the requirements of the Golden Rule. Let us simply, artlessly, and earnestly ask our Father here and now to bestow upon us in His fullness this best of all donations—the Holy Spirit.

What a royal life this is to which our Master calls us—on the one hand, deriving all our needed resources from God; and on the other hand, therefore, able to be generous and freehanded to others. "God is able to make all grace abound toward you, that ye, always having all sufficiency in all things, may abound to every good work" (2 Cor. 9:8).

Too long have we given stones when people asked for bread, and serpents where they asked for fish. We have pelted people with stones, we have stung them with the poison of asps; they have turned away from us and our Christianity with loathing. Henceforth let us go through life repeating in essence the wonderful miracle of John 6, where out of five barley loaves and two small fish, broken by the hand of the Master, and distributed by the hand of the disciples, vast crowds of hungry people were satisfied. Take your bread and fish from Christ, and then break and give— *break and give!* There will always be twelve basketsful of fragments left for your personal need.

CHAPTER TWENTY

COUNTERFEITS-BEWARE!

(Matt. 7:13-29)

The world is full of counterfeits, and shams abound! Often we paint and varnish paper to look like marble; we make paste jewels; we make the soles of boots of paper; and experts are deceived. There is great danger, therefore, of the same spirit creeping into the Church, and our Lord, who knew the hearts of people, warns His disciples against the counterfeits of true religion.

The Denial of Self

That Christian experience is a counterfeit which does not involve the denial of self. We must distinguish between the denial of self and self-denial. There may be self-denial which, instead of being the denial of self, leads to self-congratulation and self-aggrandizement. A daughter in a fashionable home may elect to forego the gossip around the afternoon tea in her mother's drawing room in order to visit an East End slum, but in her heart of hearts she may be exulting in an afternoon's freedom from conventional custom; she may be congratulating herself on the admiration which her presence may excite among the poor; she may be desirous of building up a reputation, and of extracting pity for her self-denying labors. In all this there is a subtle ministering to self which is not easy to detect, but there is no symptom of the spirit of the Cross; the Strait Gate is not entered, the Narrow Way is not trodden. The true religious spirit, which is of great price in God's sight, must cut deep into the taproot of our self-life.

Every religion has recognized this. A Hindu told me in Calcutta that Hinduism demanded eight different steps in the elimination of the self-life, beginning with the love of woman and ending with the love of money. The Greeks recited the story of the Choice of Hercules, that when his young manhood was budding he was encountered by Venus and Minerva—the former promising that she would lead him by a short and easy path to the enjoyment of all delights; while the latter, as Leonardo depicts her, demure and staid, in her dress of gray, offered him the stern tasks of duty, calling him to forego the life of self-indulgence. In Hebrew apocryphal literature there is nothing more beautiful than the sketch in the book of Esdras of the city, "full of all manner of good things," standing in the midst of a wide plain, entered by a single narrow portal, which could only be reached by crossing a narrow causeway—so narrow that only one could walk alone—with a raging fire on the right hand and storm-swept water on the left. Every religion which has touched the heart of man has bidden him to enter in by the "Strait Gate."

The Lord's picture is very graphic. Each fresh generation seems to stand in a large, open valley, full of hope and eager expectation, and each unit fully intending to make the best of the brief spell of human existence, which is all that is granted, and without the opportunity of returning for a second trial. There are two avenues by which that valley may be left; and our Lord proceeds to contrast the two gates, the character and breadth of the two ways, the number of travelers that frequent them, and their respective goals.

The Two Gates

The most popular of these two gates is a wide one that rears its lofty height in white marble, fair and glistening, whose ample space admits a never-ceasing procession of happy young forms, which fill the air with their songs and beat the earth with their dancing feet. Festoons of ivy and vine leaves are carved in the living stone, and gates that look like burnished gold stand wide. It opens on a gently sloping grassy hill, enameled with flowers and crossed by devious tracks; now and again the path expands into open spaces and woodland glades; but as furlong follows furlong the grass becomes barer, the flowers fewer, the track itself is less defined, the crowds become broken up into smaller and smaller groups, and these dissolve into individuals, until finally each finds himself alone in a land of pits and precipices, where destruction threatens at every step, while darkness which may be felt casts midnight shadows. No voice answers the voice that piteously cries for help; no hand is stretched out to catch the hand that reaches out for succor. How "wide is the gate and broad is the way that leadeth to destruction, and many there be that go in thereat" (Matt. 7:13).

But in that valley there is another aperture—a Wicket Gate, that might easily be missed unless looked for; this is so narrow that only one can enter at a time, divested of every encumbrance. The path, at the head of which this straight entrance stands, is at first steep and difficult, paved with sharp stones which cut the tender feet. It climbs the bleak hillside—on the one hand the overhanging cliffs, on the other the deep ravine, and only a ledge to walk on. It is trodden, not by crowds, but by individuals. The idea of Christiana and her children is truer in the realm of fancy than in fact. But the end is glorious, for that path breaks out at last upon the uplands, "where God Himself is Sun."

(1) *The entrance to the life of discipleship demands an effort.* Not that we need work for acceptance or forgiveness; these are ours by the free grace of God. We are not to work for salvation, but from it. We do not work to be saved; but, being saved, we work. Still there is effort to relinquish—effort to be still and to await the strong hand of our Lord, lifting us up from the brink of despair. To lay aside every weight, to refuse the tendency to self-effort, to turn one's back resolutely on some darling sin, and one's face toward the New Jerusalem, to choose the path of separation and service—these call for effort, which our Lord compares to

the passage of a Narrow Gate. You cannot drive into it in a carriage, or carry through it your moneybags and your weights.

(2) *The continuance in the path of discipleship demands continuous effort.* The world's religion is easy enough. "Do as you like" is its motto. "Be not too righteous" is its law. You may go to church, undertake some branch of religious philanthropy, and observe certain fasts and festivals—only it must be at the dictate of your own whim and be for your own self-pleasing. The path of the true disciple, on the other hand, is one of perpetual limitation and restraint. He does not do his own will, but the will of Him that sent him. He anoints his head, and washes his face, not appearing to others to fast; but all the time he is under the strict Law of Christ, which, because it is the Law of Love, is the most inexorable Law of all.

The upward path is lonely. Few there be that find it. In the times when Christianity has been most popular its real disciples have been fewest. Always it is "a little flock." Always "not many" are called. God called Abram when he was but one.

(3) *But the end is absolutely glorious,* and more than compensates. They that tread that path, saying "No" to self because they are always saying "Yes" to Christ, leave behind the valleys where the polluted air broods and climb to the upland levels of life. They do not need to wait for the end of their journey to realize God's full gift of life; but here and now, at each step and each moment, as they are faithful to death, God gives them a crown of life (Rev. 2:10); as they are delivered unto death for Jesus' sake, the life of Jesus becomes more and more manifest in their mortal bodies (2 Cor. 4:10). Each step forward is into purer atmosphere and further vision. It "leadeth unto life" (Matt. 7:14).

Real and Counterfeit Christians
That religious experience is a counterfeit which does not produce good fruit. Our Lord applies this principle, first, to false guides. It was natural that, from speaking of the Gate and Way, He should go on to characterize the Guides, who profess to be

able to guide the pilgrim feet by the right track to the right goal. He says, in effect, *Do not judge by appearances*, for they are very deceptive. The *wolf*, which comes to plunder, may don the fleece of a sheep; *thorns* may produce a little black berry, which, in the early spring, resembles the black grape; *thistles* of a certain description will have a blossom not altogether unlike the fig tree. "By their fruits ye shall know them" (Matt. 7:20).

Primarily this does not mean that the doctrine is the tree, but the person who teaches the doctrine; and you can detect his true nature, not by noticing his words and acts when he is conscious of being watched by many eyes, but by the silent and unconscious fruit of his temper, disposition, and behavior, in the privacy of the home or amid the obscurity of daily common places. A "good tree bringeth forth good fruit" (Matt. 7:17); an evil tree cannot bring forth good fruit.

But it may be replied, Are there not many among us who refuse the doctrines of the New Testament, but whose lives and characters condemn many evangelical professors? Does not the presence of such persons in our midst disprove these words of our Lord, and prove that one's life is no true test of his doctrine? No, because the very atmosphere we breathe is saturated with Christian and evangelical influences. We all owe more to our mothers than we know. The good in the persons whose case we are considering proves that they come of a godly stock, or had, like Lord Shaftesbury, a devoted governess or nurse, or came under the influence of a Christian schoolmaster. As boys they may have been taken to hear the truth as it is in Jesus, proclaimed by lips now sealed in death. To borrow the thought of another—the momentum that carries the train continues long after the driver has turned off the steam; the tidal wave moves onward long after it has left the attraction of the moon; the radiance of the dying day lingers on the horizon long after the sun has set.

On the whole, the worth and truth of the Gospel has been abundantly attested all down the ages by the myriads of noble characters it has produced, and who have been as salt to the world's corruption and as lights in its darkness

It is a solemn question for every teacher among us: "Am I bearing good or evil fruit? What is the impression which I am producing on those around me? Am I a fruit-bearing branch in the True Vine? If not, whatever my doctrine may be, I am running a serious risk of being cut down and cast into the fire." To save us from that fate, it is not enough to teach others the conditions of fruit-bearing, not enough to refrain from bearing evil fruit, not enough to be a neutral or negative quantity—the failure to bring forth good fruit will cause us to be condemned to the ax and the bonfire. Many of those who condemn others for their heterodoxy, and pride themselves on the straitness and strictness of their adherence to evangelical doctrine, but who in their criticism of others betray a terrible deficiency of Christian love, and in their domestic life give no signs of the sweetness and humility of Christ, will find someday that their fervid zeal for orthodoxy of creed, which has not been accompanied by orthodoxy of character and conduct, has not availed to secure them from the fate meted out to worthless fruit trees.

Our Lord applies the same principle, next, to false professors. He shows how far a person may go and be lost. He may have a considerable amount of reverence and respect for the Lord's name. He is depicted as addressing the Master as "Lord, Lord"; and as avowing, three times over, that the name of Christ has been the talisman and charm by the use of which all the miracles and mighty works have been accomplished (Matt. 7:22). Three classes file before us, only to be rejected at the Judgment Seat of Christ, where those eyes which are as a flame of fire pierce the counterfeit disciple through and through. First come some prophets, not in the sense of *fore*telling, but of *forth*telling, the message of a salvation which they have never appropriated for themselves. Next come the exorcists, who have cast demons out of others than themselves. Lastly come the wonder-workers. But each of these classes is turned away.

Not only does the King not know them as they approach, but He *tells* them that He never did know them, and that their works have been works of iniquity (Matt. 7:23). Every work wrought in the spirit of vainglory and for the sake of securing a personal reward is accounted as nothing by the

Master, yea, as worse than nothing—it is an affront to Him. Its doer flouts His mercy and long-suffering, and acts as though Christ had never shed His blood, never expiated his sins, never purchased his redemption. Do those who eulogize the sublime morality of this discourse, but refuse to admit the Divine claims of the Speaker, read these closing words? If so, how do they understand them? Does the sanity, which has characterized the Master's utterances hitherto, forsake Him now? Is He reliable as a Teacher and Guide only in dealing with the difficult problems of human life, and an egotist or visionary when, without any explanation or apology, He assumes the right to sit on the Judgment Seat and utter the verdict of eternity on the living and dead? If we accept the one set of utterances as the essence of truth, why should we draw the line when He speaks about making His false disciples depart?

This is He with whom you and I have to do; and, I pray you, make sure work for eternity. If you are wrong it is surely better to find out your mistake here and now rather than after the die is cast. You may speak with the tongues of men and angels, give all your goods to feed the poor, and your body to be burned in your steadfast witness to the truth—but if you are not inspired by a Divine love to God and man it will count for nothing (1 Cor. 13:1-3); and when once the Master has shut the door it will be in vain for you to stand without and knock, saying, "Open to us." The door will not open. The darkness will not be split by a shaft of ruddy light issuing from within. The stern rejection will not be succeeded by a loving recognition.

Do you fear lest such a fate should be yours? Then be of good cheer. Those that dread it most are safest from it. Those who are most self-confident have most reason for alarm. "Not everyone that *saith* unto Me, Lord, Lord, shall enter into the Kingdom of Heaven, but he that *doeth* the will of My Father which is in heaven" (Matt. 7:21). There is no need to die before we enter it; but here and now, as we with many fears and failures set ourselves to do God's will, we may enter the kingdom and become citizens of its metropolis—the New Jerusalem which comes down out of heaven from God being radiant with His glory.

A Faith that Leads to Obedience

That religious experience is counterfeit which does not secure contact between the soul and Christ with a faith leading to obedience. In any of those Syrian valleys, which some have visited, between Beirut and Damascus, it is possible to see wrought out the closing picture of His sermon. In the summer the soil is baked and hard with the intense heat, and any spot will serve equally well as the site of a house. No one can say whether his neighbor has built well or ill; and only the builder himself knows.

But in the winter all is altered. The country is then exposed to sudden and heavy storms. The stiff breeze drives up the rain clouds from the Mediterranean, which empty themselves in floods of rain, and suddenly the channels, which for months had been little better than heaps of stones, are filled with foaming floods from bank to small hills, pouring down into the valleys and carrying all before them.

It goes ill, under such circumstances, with a person who has pitched his slightly constructed house on the sand, taking no heed to dig down to the rock beneath, for the foundations are sapped by the rushing torrent, and the very sand is swept into new banks and beds. But a builder who has excavated to the living rock, and grappled it in the lowest courses of his construction, can look without dismay at the scene of devastation around. It comes not nigh to him; only with his eyes does he behold and see the doom of the unwary (Matt. 7:24-27).

Such is the contrast between the man who hears and does not heed, and him who hears, ponders, and obeys. For, in the words of the Apostle, "Not the hearers of the Law are just before God, but the doers of the Law shall be justified" (Rom. 2:13).

What searching words are these! We have all heard, but have we done? Are we hearers that forget, or doers that work? Do we continue in the perfect Law of Liberty? Have we ever come into personal and living contact with that Stone, that tried Stone, that precious Cornerstone, which God has laid before the worlds were made, for a sure foundation?

To believe about Christ is not enough; we must believe in Him. We must come to Him as the Living Stone, and be made living stones (1 Peter 2:4-8). Then, and in the impulses received from Him through the Holy Spirit, we shall proceed to build the structure of a godly and holy character, not with wood, hay, and stubble, but with gold, silver, and precious stones, and it shall grow unto a holy temple in the Lord (1 Cor. 3:10-15).

Is it to be wondered at that the people felt that the Master's words were fraught with a mysterious authority and power which were absent from the words of all other speakers? Many have borne witness to this same characteristic, which adds the greater condemnation to those who reject, but which communicates the pulse and thrill of the Divine Spirit to those who receive with meekness the engrafted word that is able to save their souls (James 1:21).